PENGUIN BOOKS
LOOKING FOR MAYA

Atima Srivastava was born in Mumbai and moved to London when she was eight. *Looking for Maya* is her second novel.

LOOKING FOR MAYA

ATIMA SRIVASTAVA

PENGUIN BOOKS

Penguin Books India (P) Ltd., 11 Community Centre, Panchsheel Park, New Delhi
110017, India
Penguin Books Ltd., 27 Wrights Lane, London W8 5TZ, UK
Penguin Putnam Inc., 375 Hudson Street, New York, NY 10014, USA
Penguin Books Australia Ltd., Ringwood, Victoria, Australia
Penguin Books Canada Ltd., 10 Alcorn Avenue, Suite 300, Toronto, Ontario MAV 3B2, Canada
Penguin Books (NZ) Ltd., 182-190 Wairau Road, Auckland 10, New Zealand

First published in Great Britain by Quartet Books Limited 1999
First published in India by Penguin Books India 1999

The author would like to thank the Arts Council for financial support during the writing of
this work.

This is a work of fiction. Names, characters, places and incidents are either the product of
the author's imagination or are used fictitiously, and any resemblance to actual persons,
living or dead, events, or locales is entirely coincidental.

Printed at Chaman Enterprises, Delhi

maya: *mah-ya* (Hindi) *n.* illusion

The body dies
again and again
The mind does not
Nor does Maya
Illusion lives on
mind lives on
Kabir says, hopes and desires don't die

Kabir

for my parents of course,
and in memory
of
my grandmother

Sipping an espresso, I stretched out my legs in the sunlight. All around me, people were babbling in different languages, students, tourists. The waiter in his crisp apron carried precarious coffees to the tables set on the pavement. Behind me, I could hear the Italian football on the big screen inside the café and I felt inexplicably happy. The final examinations were over, the long summer yawned before me and I had a feeling that I was going to live and live. There was another café opposite on Greek Street, where people in sunglasses were sitting sipping coffees, but Bar Italia was still the original café in Soho. It stayed open till three in the morning when people emerged from Ronnie Scott's jazz club across the road. They were served hot coffee and croissants and sweet cakes. Maison Bertaux, the old French *pâtisserie* was a hundred yards away, the black hairdressers with old-fashioned chrome chairs and durex machine, the Pakistani newsagent that sold European papers, the Polish lunch bar full of old men in cravats. I'd told Luke all about the corners of London, full of different cultures, introduced him proudly to places that he had only heard about as he was growing up by the sea.

I felt his arm sliding around my shoulders. He nuzzled the side of his head lovingly against my neck and the newly cut hair bristled against my skin. And suddenly, it occurred to me that I hadn't been aware of Luke for these delicious minutes of knowing I was living in my beautiful city. I moved my head to take a look as he slipped easily into the chair next to mine.

'Looks great,' I smiled, rubbing my thumb against the side of his head, like the fur on a cat.

'It's an amazing place. Just like you said. A real barber's shop. Faded signed photographs from the fifties and everything,' he said generously, smiling at me.

I knew how much he loved me. I'd known it since we'd met at the beginning of our final year. We'd come together finally, having seen each other moving around campus with different groups, with other people, until at last, (we liked to say), met at the right time. Of all the places for students to meet, we had met in the library. Of course I had noticed him before, it was impossible not to. Luke had one of those faces that couldn't be described without the word honest slotted in somewhere. His smile was dazzling, his eyes clear and blue and twinkling. He was handsome like anything, serious and eager and keen. He had put down his books and asked me for a cigarette, our conversation easily staggering into the information: what subject, where do you live, what sort of music. The lights had gone out and we'd said goodbye, almost immediately bumping into each other again in the coffee bar, and then again in the square. We couldn't stop smiling that day, soaking each other in, feeling exuberant, sitting in the Union bar till it closed too, and already knowing each other.

The university was in an old shipbuilding town with no romantic spots. We drove down in Luke's old Saab to the harbour to see the sunset, stayed till moonlight, unwilling to let each other out of sight. He liked old things, old cars and old ideas, despised Englishness and its restrictions, loved music and its egalitarianism. He held my hand and looked into my face. We had leaned into a kiss and the kiss had gone on for hours, a silent rushing journey through the stars. Lost in space. At the end of the kiss, we had come to the heart of each other, gasping for breath, exhilarated with the moon and the world and everything.

'I want to know all about you. Everything and still keep going, never get to the end of it,' he'd said, his bright blue eyes shining.

'I feel like I've known you for ever. And there's so much I want to show you,' I'd said, both of us so wrapped up in the deep romance of it, unaware that people everywhere say such things and believe them to be unique.

Luke was my first real boyfriend. Almost immediately we had fallen into the patterns of a life together, enjoying the shopping, the cooking, the TV, essay writing. Friends who shared the same bed. The ease with which we spent the last stage of our formal education together, made it the best time of my life. He didn't know about the Kings Road or the Marquee in Wardour Street or about jumping the trains without a ticket and I had gleefully filled in his gaps of knowledge. We had hitched into London on weekends, bought leopardskin trousers and Spotlight hair dye, watched bands in dark smoky clubs and kissed on the last train back. Sometimes, Luke's open admiration for my fake cosmopolitan experience made me uneasy but I admired him too, for all he'd shown me: which knife in a restaurant, the recreational use of soft drugs, the window into his life at public school. We had become a couple on campus, a couple people liked to look at. I knew he liked it less than I, for him our relationship was beyond that, it was close and deep. Yet, it was enjoyable to be looked at together. We were lithe and attractive, my dark skin against his pale skin, his hair blond, mine dark. Our arms were always wrapped around each other making a creature which was IndianEnglish. Luke liked that phrase I had coined as my own, although I had stolen it from Indian cinema magazines which had gossip columns in that strange hybrid language full of Indian words written in English italics. We had given it another meaning, my white boyfriend and his dusky damsel.

Luke consulted his watch and grimaced. 'We'll have to go soon. I said I'd meet Ralph after lunch.'

I nodded, leaning my head back on the chair, feeling the sunshine pressing on my skin. Luke called both his parents by their first names and although I'd said RaviKavi in my head, and even for fun sometimes, I could never get used to calling my parents by the pet name their friends had for them.

'Ralph's having lunch with an old friend. From the old days. We won't stay long,' said Luke, pulling on a cigarette. We were both watching the street through our sunglasses. It amused me how Luke regarded family obligation as a chore, even though he only ever had to see his mum and dad at Christmas and birthdays and occasional times when one of them was in town. Even when I'd left home and started living sixty miles from London, RaviKavi expected full weekly reports and fortnightly meetings with me. Their eager questionnaires hadn't changed since I'd been at school, excavating the English world on their behalf. What did they give you to eat at dinner, my dad would ask, what do you mean they only seasoned the chops with salt and pepper?

'Excuse me,' said a woman with a camera in her hands, stopping by our table. 'Do you mind if I take a photograph of you?'

Luke and I looked at each other without taking off our sunglasses and smiled broadly.

'I'm from *Pinned* magazine, we're doing a photo spread of Londoners. Interesting looking people,' she smiled.

I felt a surge of love for Luke, at how beautiful he must look to her, and me next to him, beautiful by association. It had never been anything passionate, we had fitted together like spoons, admiring each other like complementary things. Horse and carriage, bread and cheese.

The photographer asked us both to lean towards the camera, and at the last minute Luke threw his arm around me and pulled me close. He wanted to say, 'It's not just a pose, it's incidental this superficial beauty, there's more to it than that.' For Luke the long kiss at the harbour was always a point of reference, a feeling he liked to revive between us, but it seemed to me that that heat, that white intensity had cooled to blood temperature, to a level where we now lived contentedly and peacefully. She took my address, as I was the one with an address in London and said she'd send us the magazine.

'We'll be late,' said Luke paying the waiter. Suddenly, I didn't want to meet Ralph or his friend, I wanted to push Luke into a doorway crowded with cardboard boxes and oil drums, kiss him long and hard on the lips against the barrage of noise and colour in my sweet city, in my wonderful world.

Ralph was sitting with his old friend at a table inside the cool elegance of a small restaurant in Meard Mews. Shadows passed over them from the large window facing the garrulous street. Ralph stood up as he saw us arrive, our frayed shorts and sandalled feet stepping upon the thick carpet. The chill of the air conditioning hit me like a slap and I shivered. I liked Ralph, I'd met him twice and I knew how well he approved of me. I realized with a shock that his friend at the table looking at us diligently, was Indian. He was wearing a pale linen jacket with an open shirt and his hair was thick and wavy, flopping over one bushy eyebrow, and he had a shaggy moustache which covered his top lip. On his nose rested thin metal-framed John Lennon – my father would have said Gandhiji – glasses. How typical of Luke to have not mentioned it. English people never thought it quite correct to point out racial difference, thought it vulgar to assume that an Indian should be interested or even know another Indian in a big city. RaviKavi were obsessed with it, always nosing out connections, however tenuous, to mark their country and their long journey. Arrey, my dad would say to a complete stranger, are you related to the Mehtas in Allahabaad, then you are almost my neighbour, you will be insulting me by not coming to my house for khaana.

Ralph shook Luke's hand and gave me a little hug and pulled out a chair for me. His friend was looking at me curiously and I remember thinking, he's old, but he's quite handsome. For a moment I wasn't sure that he was Indian, because his skin was so fair, the colour of pale golden tobacco and his eyes were grey more than brown. I didn't know Indians could have grey eyes.

'Amrit, this is Luke, I think you remember my errant son, and this is his lovely friend, Mira,' said Ralph expansively. 'Amrit Kaushik, Mira Chowdhary.'

'Hello,' said Amrit looking at both of us. 'So nice to see you.'

'Good grief!' said Ralph, taking in Luke's appearance. 'Is this a new fashion?'

Luke smiled and exhaled smoke. 'Yeah, it's a new fashion, Ralph.'

'Two earrings?' said Ralph doubtfully. 'One earring, alright, although in our day, that meant something else altogether.'

'In Indian villages, lots of men wear two earrings, it doesn't mean they're doubly homosexual,' said Luke and I sucked in my lips in order not to laugh. I noticed a smile creeping around Amrit's face. Ralph looked crushed.

'London is, after all, only a village,' smiled Amrit. 'And our days are over, Ralph.' We all laughed. 'Now,' he said, cleverly changing the subject, 'would you like something to drink? Or perhaps a dessert. They're rather good here.'

We said we'd have some wine and coffee and Amrit looked at the menu and ordered a bottle of Chardonnay. I looked around the restaurant at the waiters standing in shadows and the murmuring diners and I crossed my legs underneath the weight of the thick damask tablecloth. His accent was Indian, but not like any Indian accent I had ever heard. It was Indian but it was posh, there was no confusion of Ws pronounced as Vs, a distinction that my father after spending twenty years in England still couldn't discern. His accent wasn't like my father's lumbering careful English, a language he always seemed to be getting over and done with before he could luxuriate in his perfectly modulated Hindi. It wasn't like Mr Ahmed the ticket collector at the station who had always had plenty to say in English and Urdu about the colours I had dyed my hair at the age of sixteen. Amrit's accent wasn't like the blacked-up Benny Hill, or Peter Sellers or the Sabu character in the old black and white movies. He didn't sound like the Visiting Gods who came to stay in their hordes with RaviKavi and pronounced Cambridge as Kambridge, snacks as snakes.

The waiter showed Amrit the bottle and poured a little into his glass. Amrit smiled and said softly, 'I'm sure it's fine,' and gestured towards my glass. It struck me as supremely sophisticated to not even bother to taste the wine, because if it wasn't very expensive, what did it matter? It was mere affectation. I thought with shame of how I had dragged Tash into a restaurant in London, to show off what I had learnt from Luke, sipped a glass of cheap wine with a serious expression on my face.

'Hmmm, yes I think I do remember you,' Luke was saying and so I looked at him and then at Amrit, as though legitimately. 'Once, in the holidays.'

'Kids,' said Ralph.

'I tried to teach you chess. You weren't terribly interested. But then you were a dreaded teenager,' smiled Amrit. He didn't look at me.

Luke began to smoke and smiled back at Amrit politely.

'Would you pass the ashtray, Ralph?' he said.

Within five seconds of meeting Ralph, Luke became formal, a little resentful at being his father's son. It seemed to be their way of relating to each other, this over-formality and I supposed it was how all boys who had been to public school sat with their fathers. There were no excited howls of 'hello' and 'ahh' on the phone between them, as there were between me and my parents who drove me mad the way they treated every word,every contact from me as a national holiday.

'And how are you, Mira? How are things with you?' said Ralph, leaning across to me with a genial smile.

I shrugged. 'OK, I haven't done much about anything. I suppose I should think about getting a job.'

'You must talk to Amrit,' said Ralph suddenly. 'He's a writer too.'

I cringed. I had won a short-story competition some months ago, won a hundred pounds, blown it on a weekend to Spain with Luke, who had boasted to everybody about his girlfriend the writer. RaviKavi had smiled knowingly on the phone. Of course I was going to be a writer eventually, despite the degree in History; it was in our genes. Never mind that RaviKavi hadn't written for twenty years, left their literary friends behind in Delhi and Bombay, lost all the books they had published, dismissed the mark they had each made on the landscape of Hindi poetry.

'Oh, god, it's nothing. Nothing really. Of no consequence,' I said with embarrassment as Luke and Ralph explained.

'All writers begin from no consequences,' grinned Amrit.

'Mira's parents are both poets,' said Ralph proudly, even though he had never met my parents, never heard them reciting their poems about rural India and democracy and open skies to the Visiting Gods who stayed in the house and belched their way through the London itineraries prepared by my parents.

'Really?' said Amrit turning towards me. 'What are their names?'

I smiled. It was such an Indian question. English people asked your name out of politeness and necessity, but for an Indian your surname signified everything they needed to know about where you came from, what sort of background, even what your profession was. When I was growing up, the stubborn point in our little triangular family, I used to think Indian people walked about with maps rolled up under their arms, ready to pinpoint each other, label them and talk of them, in the stereotypes they had unearthed. Arrey, he is a Gujju, don't expect a discount...Delhi has full-eee degenerated under this pushy Punjabi culture...of course he is a scholar, Bengalis have always been...

Amrit hadn't heard of Ravi Chowdhary or Kavita Joshi, but he nodded just the same, and I was aware that I wanted to tell him, wanted him to know where I was from, which meant explaining where RaviKavi were from. He knew Lucknow, how civilized the people were in that small town where my parents had grown up speaking that gorgeous language referred to as Hindustani, the mix of Urdu and Hindi reminiscent of the Nawabs of Oudh.

'You know what they say about Kayastas?' said Amrit with a smile. 'This caste you belong to, the writers' caste. This odd fifth caste. They began as scribes in the Mughal empire and imbibed the ways of the Muslims. My father used to say, never trust a Kayasta, they are sharaabi kebabis. They drink and eat meat, they are nearly Muslims themselves!'

We all burst out laughing and I felt an odd kinship with him because he knew these things.

'I thought Muslims didn't drink?' said Luke ingenuously.

'They're not supposed to drink,' I said shyly. 'But their music and literature...'

'Hindus are a pious lot,' declared Amrit and smiled.

'The fifth caste?' asked Luke in puzzlement.

'See, they are neither priests, nor warriors, nor merchants. Nor are they the "Children of God",' Amrit smiled. 'They are side-ys.'

I laughed out loud at his use of the euphemism for Untouchability, at his use of Bollywood slang for hooligans.

'But surely,' insisted Luke, 'the caste system isn't relevant any more? Not amongst educated, urban people?'

'Indeed, indeed,' said Amrit, with such a show of innocence, that I wanted to laugh again.

He didn't have intimate knowledge of the world of Hindi literature but he knew how I had learnt my language, from the privileged position of the daughter of poets amongst traders and clerks and bank managers. He knew in the way, I realized with a sudden shock, Luke or Ralph would never know. His Hindi pronunciation was accented. He must be an English writer, I remember thinking.

'And your parents, do they live here too?' asked Amrit.

'They've gone back to India, because my grandad died and my dad had to sort out the house and then they went to Delhi because they're trying to build a house there on a plot they bought years ago,' I said in a rush.

I wondered if he knew automatically the freedom enshrined in those words. If he could imagine how my heart had soared at their worried faces at Terminal 3, when they were leaving me behind, all alone, unheard of, free as a bird. How I had reassured them that I would be fine, I would look in on their house regularly, I would manage very well in the flat they had recently purchased in an uncharacteristic burst of investment. I would thrive on the monthly allowance they had arranged with my bank. RaviKavi had never planned their lives, looked down their noses at money. They had moved from their small town to big cities but always lived frugally, enjoying their own community of two, never making any real friends in this country, inviting all the old ones to come and complete and redraw the circle of Delhi–Bombay–London.

'I've been living independently for nearly three years anyway, Dad, what's the problem?' I'd said confidently and RaviKavi had frowned at each other.

'We'll speak every week. You keep all your doors locked. We'll be back soon,' my dad had threatened me. 'Soon' had turned into months, because land plots couldn't be abandoned, building work couldn't be left unsupervised in Delhi, which was lawless these days, so their blue aerogrammes had explained.

'Take as long as you want,' I'd said generously, already seeing my brilliant future spreading before me like a glittering universe.

'Don't be funny,' my mother had admonished.

RaviKavi hadn't any need to say don't do anything to excess, don't be a bad girl, don't make us ashamed of you. Lucknow people didn't speak directly, it was vulgar. In the Mughal times, the pattern of conversation had been full of incredible politenesses, delightfully archaic phrases that my father had often regaled me with. When the cultured Muslims went to enquire after a friend's health, they didn't rudely ask, 'Are you unwell?' They would say, 'I hear those who wish you ill, are unwell.'

'Ralph tells me you're off to foreign parts?' said Amrit, neatly changing the subject from me to Luke and I was glad of it.

'I'm planning a trip to India,' said Luke enthusiastically, absently slipping his hand across the table over mine. I couldn't help feeling a mixture of elation and embarrassment whenever Luke demonstrated affection towards me in front of either of his parents. They had thought nothing of Luke and me sleeping together in the spare room in their house in Brighton, twenty minutes from the front. Somehow, despite his Englishness, I was conscious of Amrit's eyes upon us, just like I had always been fearful of 'uncles' and 'aunties' roaming the Pizza Parades and Chix Chox of my childhood in North London. Any boys I knew then had been strictly instructed by me that kissing and cuddling was naff in public. I had yearned to snog on pavements, suck tongues on the bus, but the humiliation of my parents' certain disappointment had been too much to bear. University had been the site of permissiveness, safely sixty miles from uncles and aunties and Lucknow sensibilities.

'Luke's researching the musical influences of the East upon the Western tradition,' said Ralph, and Amrit raised his eyebrows.

'I'm waiting for a grant from the Arts Council, it should be enough for a few months,' said Luke. 'There's an international artists' community on the edge of Delhi. It's a sort of cultural centre, multi-disciplined. I want to go and stay there.'

Amrit nodded and smiled. 'Yes, I met the fellow who runs it, Prem Nath, at the Royal Festival Hall last summer. I was doing a reading there. You remember, Ralph, when we saw the Bach recital?'

I looked at Amrit talking so knowledgeably about so many things and I thought how clever he is, and then I looked into my wine.

'He's a really fascinating person,' said Luke, 'and actually an accomplished musician himself, a tabla player. He was extremely supportive and it's an area that hasn't really been touched upon. I'm interested in the wandering troubadours; they still practise their craft, in almost exactly the same way, the making of the instruments, the oral tradition, the movements, they're still intact.' Luke looked up sheepishly and I smiled at him because he reminded me of an absent-minded professor whenever he talked about his work, oblivious to everyone around him. Ralph and Amrit were listening with serious faces.

'Luke's worked very hard,' said Ralph softly, looking at his watch. He was really proud of Luke, I knew that, but Luke never seemed to notice. They were so alike in many ways, so warm and tender to everyone and so diffident with each other. Two people who kept missing each other the whole time, substituting the loss of communication with barbed comments.

'Yeah,' I grinned and made a face. 'Luke's a real swot.'

Luke grinned back at me and held my stare. And I thought with a start, that my opinion was the only one at the table that interested him, that I was the person who mattered to him most. I looked away hurriedly and drank down the glass.

'Luke, you haven't forgotten Mum's birthday?' said Ralph. 'We're having a do. You'll bring Mira, of course?'

Luke clicked his tongue in exasperation. 'Of course I haven't forgotten. I thought I'd get her a line drawing of the Pier, I saw one in Charing Cross Road of all places. Pen and ink. It's quite old.'

'Yes, she'd like that,' said Ralph.

I leant my elbow on the table, cupping my chin, and thought how formal they were and how estranged I was from Luke's life. And I had an odd feeling of utter happiness as though one could always be free from another person's spleen and blood and manners. I was conscious of Amrit sitting opposite me and I wondered if he too felt like an outsider, an Indian amongst English people and happy to be there, intact in himself.

'I'm sorry,' said Ralph, reaching for his wallet, 'I really have to go. I have to make an auction by three and I'll be driving back. Luke, I did say two o'clock.'

'Never mind, Dad,' said Luke. 'Give my love to Mum. I'll phone her in the next couple of days.'

'Let me,' said Amrit, placing a finger on Ralph's sleeve.

'OK,' said Ralph cheerfully. 'Sorry I can't make the launch. Too hectic.'

Amrit waved it off good naturedly and then he turned to us. 'If you're free, you're welcome to come along. It would be nice to have some young people there. There'll be some wine and some boring speeches but you might find it amusing,' he said.

'Amrit's new book is just about to come out,' explained Ralph. 'I hope at least, Luke, you can come up with some suitable...'

'Come as you are, both of you,' grinned Amrit. 'Don't be so stuffy, Ralph.'

They laughed like old friends. I looked at Luke who was smoking as he leant back in his chair, a resolute expression set on his face. Amrit smiled and pushed an invitation across the tablecloth towards me and as my fingers touched upon the slim card, I saw his eyes rising to look into mine.

'It would be nice to see you, Luke,' said Amrit. 'I'd like to hear some more about your obsessions. Both of you.'

CHAPTER TWO

As usual, Luke was quiet afterwards. I squeezed his hand as we entered Soho Square from one of its four pathways. Office workers in shirt sleeves and despatch riders in thick leather armour were scattered on the grass munching sandwiches. A radio was playing pop music. Pigeons waddled around the central construction, a building with a slanting roof and small windows.

'It looks like a little house, what d'you think it is?' I asked Luke as we approached it.

'Some fucking English monument built by some rich bastard,' said Luke.

'Why d'you let Ralph make you feel like this?' We flopped down on the grass. 'We were late. He was busy. He doesn't mean to be like you think he is.' I was stroking Luke's face.

He placed his hand over mine and closed his eyes, breathed in as though fresh air was on ration. 'I know,' he said quietly. 'Thanks.'

I stretched out beside him, my legs parallel to his, our bodies so close. I didn't want to talk about Ralph or the invitation or anything else. I wanted to move about languidly in the dry grass and listen to the music and feel the feeling of happiness pouring from the blue sky. This spell of good weather, how good it was, I wanted to say, how unexpected, how grey London would become as soon as it rained, like a ravishing woman curling into an old grey crone. I wanted to squeeze the life out of the sun, eat life, soar above the clouds. There was a restlessness in the pit of my stomach. But at these times, I felt myself needed by Luke, usually so capable and sure, these times when he felt like the little boy who was made to eat turnips and spinach and not allowed to leave the table till he had finished. I liked him needing me. I thought it was close to love, not as close as passion, but a good thing, a brave thing, to allow yourself to need and be needed.

'Ah, forget it. Ralph's not my problem any more,' said Luke and turned over to lie on his stomach, putting an arm across my chest. I could see the burnished hair on his lower arm, sense the heat of his body, the smell I knew every shade of.

'What d'you think of Amrit?' said Luke speaking into the grass, blowing at the green shards through his nostrils.

I was staring at the blue sky. Was it true that if you looked straight at the sun you would go blind because the Sun God disallowed such nerve? Or was that something I had heard, something between fact and fiction? I didn't want to look at the sun in any case, I would snub it. I wanted to feel the blue, the universe of blue.

'He was alright,' I said. 'Did you really not remember him?'

'Sort of,' mumbled Luke and then he spun around and lay on his back, smoked at the sky, grinning. 'He's at that age. When men have to start shagging young women.'

'You'll be that age one day. Is he?'

'Oh, yeah,' drawled Luke at the sky, drawing out the disdain with his words. 'He's got loads of women, loads of kids, I dunno, some sort of weird life. He's the type. I'll never be like that. I'll love you for ever in time.' He said the last sentence with a laugh, trying to laugh off the longing as he turned to look at me, pressed his mouth into mine.

'What type?' I said, my lips wet with his.

'Oh, you know,' he shrugged. Then: 'You know Ralph had an affair once?'

'He didn't!' I exclaimed, shocked at the fact and outraged at Luke's casual revelation of it.

'It was years ago. So pathetic. He thought he was going to change his life. He got all rigorous about it. Left home to shack up with her. Someone always gets hurt, he said to Mum. She was devastated, and he couldn't even see how stupid he looked, like an adolescent.'

I giggled. At school I used to wish RaviKavi would divorce and make my life interesting. I'd never then heard of people having affairs, not outside of American soap operas, all impossibly delicious and exotic. I thought about Ralph and his genial smile and Luke's mum, Matty, so nice and pale with her eyelids blinking.

'Who was it, the other woman?' I said, sitting up.

'Some girl.'

'Why do you think Amrit's like that?' I asked. It was a stupid question, because at the back of it I was thinking faintly that Indians weren't like that, degenerate like English people. That was RaviKavi speaking, their legacy, their sniggering over the values of English people, their belief in their own intact world of decency.

'Why not?' said Luke. 'Same generation. Same slackness.'

I giggled at the London words Luke had picked up.

'Didn't you notice the way he was looking at you?'

'At me?' I said, feeling hot all over.

Luke laughed. 'He was gagging for it,' he said, and I punched him playfully.

'Don't be disgusting,' I laughed. 'I couldn't believe it when you said "doubly homosexual" in front of Ralph!'

'Nearly blew a gasket,' chuckled Luke.

'You wore them deliberately,' I said, shaking my head, but Luke's mood had changed to seriousness.

'Mira,' he said quietly after we lay back, breathing in

spurts, smiling at the sun, 'the letter I wrote...'

'It was gorgeous,' I whispered.

'I meant everything in it.'

Just before the exams he had passed me a note under my door, having left me alone to revise. It was short and emotional. It told me how glad he was that we loved each other and how he would be nowhere without me and all I'd taught him. I had liked it so much. I had imagined that perhaps we were like RaviKavi, or that one day we would be like them, standing in love, not having to snog in public over it, knowing and loving each other because of our shared knowledge. But I knew we didn't have a shared knowledge. What Luke and I had was our differences and the experiences we had gone through in the last year, the movies we'd seen and the bed we'd shared. We were constantly in touch with the differences; it fascinated us, this lack of sameness. I felt suddenly disheartened, remembering waiting for him outside Bar Italia under the blue sky and the yellow sun and the foreign world, and how I had not given him a single thought, felt myself to be utterly, deliciously alone, and revelled in it.

'I'm going out with the Sunbeam and the Oily Rag tonight. Guys night out. Wanna come? Shall we go home first?'

My flat, the flat RaviKavi had tremblingly poured their life savings into as an investment, had become a kind of sub home for Luke and me, although Luke had his own place on the other side of London, a squat he was sharing with two other ex-students. We'd made a point not to move in together, especially as Luke needed a lot of space for his work and because I didn't like the idea of deceiving RaviKavi, although I had already been deceiving them for a year about how friendly I was with my friend Luke. I had a feeling they knew, but realized it wasn't sordid or horrible or temporary, and were waiting for me to say something officially.

'I don't like the Sunbeam,' I said with a frown. 'He's dirty. He never has a bath. And that scar under his eye, like he was cut in a fight...'

'He's an amazing guy,' said Luke. 'He knows engines.'

'Why's everything amazing, everybody amazing!' I said, suddenly irritated by his good nature. The Sunbeam was half-Armenian as well as disfigured. 'Why d'you like... everybody so much?' I had been about to say ethnic people, black people, people who are not English but it wasn't fair or true. Luke had started his investigation of Eastern music long before we had come together, although sometimes I wondered if I was part of the research. Of course I knew this was pure belligerence, some expression of righteousness expected by black students at our right-on university where Black Politics was in vogue. Neither I, nor anybody in my family had a single musical bone in our bodies. My mother had never got the hang of the sitar and the nearest we ever got to good music were some ten-rupee tapes of Mehndi Hassan singing gazals, that my parents had owned since they left Bombay for London.

'Sorry,' said Luke in an injured tone. I knew he was hurt. God, it was so easy to hurt him, sometimes it scared me.

'I just can't handle disfigured people,' I said deliberately, and we both laughed. 'I keep staring at him. Why doesn't he wear sunglasses?' I demanded and Luke grinned.

'Wearing sunglasses at home is the kind of fashion statement only London trendies make. Even disfigured people aren't that desperate,' he said and we laughed again.

'Shut up,' I said, pretending to be offended, glad I'd turned it around.

'Why don't you go to the thing?'

'Not without you,' I said hotly.

'Yeah, go on. It'll give him a thrill. And anyway, I need to go home first. There's some research I want to do.'

'You're going to leave me in town by myself?' I wailed. Luke was one of those people who loved studying, even now we'd done with studying. When I had met him in the library he was carrying out a pile of books and I was loitering in the lobby smoking.

'It's your town,' said Luke, turning to face me with a wink.

'Anyway, these things are always better at the beginning. All the drink runs out. They're not like real parties. Everyone goes from work.'

'Oh,' I said. 'How do you know? No, I'd feel funny.'

'You should. You'll see what you've got to look forward to when you write your bestseller. Loadsamoney. Publishers creeping about, journalists, you'll love it.'

'Do you think that's why I want to write?' I said, propping myself up on my elbow.

'Only blockheads write for anything but money, that's what Samuel Johnson said, wasn't it?' said Luke.

I smiled, because it was I who had begun Luke's introduction to London with the famous words about being tired of London and being tired of life. He'd grown up in Brighton, he'd only seen London on day trips and then only the London of tourists. I had shown him the pockets of London that he had never imagined could be true. The little countries inside the capital. I'd taken him to Wembley full of aspiring Gujeratis in Mercs, to Green Lanes dotted with Cypriots sitting in darkened rooms playing cards, Finsbury Park thrumming with Nigerian taxi drivers who said, 'I dhink I no you from somewhere, befour.' The Spanish tapas bar in Camden Town, the Jewish bagel bakery in Golders Green, the Irish fish and chips in The Free Republic of County Archway. 'How come we never cross the river?' Luke had asked. 'What river?' I'd said. There was only North London and Soho. All the rest, the West and the East and the South, was all propaganda.

'You should go,' said Luke, 'he invited you.'

'He invited us,' I said.

'Hmm,' smiled Luke. 'Listen, will you come and look at the print? Tell me what you think?'

'Of course I will.' I sighed and lay back on the grass.

We let the sunlight pour on our faces and inhaled the green smell of freshly-cut grass and listened to the machine trundling around the square spraying the grass confetti in its wake. After some time we walked into Charing Cross Road from a side street. I was feeling faint from the heat, gasping for breath as we strode along together, our bare legs brushing occasionally.

The ancient shop was full of dusty maps and piles of secondhand books. It reminded me too much of RaviKavi's house to be as interesting as it was to Luke. The house I had grown up in was full of bookshelves erected without a plumbline by my father, and filled with the books they had brought from India. The library was enriched every time we made a trip home or the Visiting Gods came to stay. Their books weren't nicely arranged in flowing colours and authorship, they were all shapes and sizes, covers made from cardboard and cloth, falling apart at the seams and webbed spines, pushed pell-mell in front of each other, squashed and hidden by double rows.

'Look.' He blinked as he showed me the collection of fine drawings. I traced my finger over the cellophane covering the Pier and the Pavilion. He bought two, one for me to hang up in the flat.

'Go with Frank. Phone him up,' said Luke.

'Frank doesn't read books, he won't like it,' I said dismissively, even though Frank had probably read more books than I, despite the fact that he hadn't been to university. I had met him at my first gig (Bad Manners, Electric Ballroom) when I was just sixteen. He had saved me from a fight that was breaking out between skinheads, and although we were the same age I regarded him as my older brother. I'd been on holiday with him and he had come up to stay with me for several weekends, before and after I had got together with Luke.

'Maybe I will,' I added quickly.

'Wait for the bus with me,' said Luke and we walked back towards Tottenham Court Road. I glanced into Foyles on the way and wondered if Amrit's books were on the shelf in there.

'What does Amrit write about?' I said.

Luke shrugged. 'Dunno. Probably quite high-brow stuff.

The Cultural Diaspora, literary criticism; he teaches too.'

I had taken a Literature option in my final year called Post Colonial Literature and studied Naipaul and Rushdie and Desai, been given lots of A3 photocopied articles on Race Deconstruction, which I'd used to line my underwear drawers with. I hadn't attended many of the lectures either, intimidated by the earnest class and the amount of background reading required. I'd gained my degree by the skin of my teeth.

We waited outside BurgerKing for a number 30. It was a quarter to five. The invitation was for six-thirty, in a restaurant in Dean Street.

'I'll call you tomorrow,' said Luke, 'I might have to go and meet some people in the evening. What will you do, walk around?'

'Yeah,' I shrugged. 'Look in the shops. I might not even bother to go. Take my print so it's safe. Bring it tomorrow.'

'OK. Take care,' said Luke in the little voice he used whenever we said goodbye.

I watched the bus trundle away and when the next bus came, jumped on without thinking, flashing my travel card at the driver. I raced upstairs and made, as I always did, for the front right-hand seat. 'Look Dad,' I used to say when we went shopping on the 52 all the way to Ealing Road for Indian vegetables, before he finally passed his test, 'look, I'm driving the bus.' 'Stop bouncing, the driver will get a headache.' I watched the number 30 turn the corner and then stared out of the window. I'd have to be quick if I was going to shower, change and come back into town in under two hours. I bit my lip and looked at the invitation. It was a plain white rectangle, nice thick paper. It said Amrit Kaushik's latest book *The Journey of One of Many* was to be launched at 6.30 p.m.

As soon as I turned the key to the flat, the phone rang and an arrow of guilt shot through me. I debated whether to pick it up or not. After all, there were a number of reasons that I could have gone home first. I was irritated with myself for being so devious over nothing at all. I grabbed the phone.

'I haven't phoned to chat.'

I giggled. 'Hey, Frankie. What's going on?'

'Listen, I've booked the tickets, OK?'

'Frank!' I laughed. 'It's August! We're not going till New Year. What's the big rush?'

'That's how much you know about booking holidays, Miss Student,' he teased. 'Anyway, I had to arrange the time off. I did it on the company plastic, got a special deal. We'll drive down to the airport. It's a great flight, I had to pay a bit extra to get it, but no way I'm taking some ridiculous 6 a.m. flight, yeah?'

'Yeah, yeah,' I said. I knew Frank's holiday started the minute he left the house. He didn't like having anything less than luxury. I'd been on holiday with him twice, and now I had got the hang of it. We always drove to the airport or got someone to drive us, and the last time Frank had managed to phone up some dilapidated taxi firm in Portugal to pick us up at the airport. We collapsed laughing at the old man holding up a bedraggled cardboard sign with a shakily handwritten Markovitz and Chowdhary falling off the end. Frank had gleefully organized the whole thing because although he didn't have that sort of money or job, he'd always wanted to be met like an executive.

'Is Luke jealous?' asked Frank mischievously.

'Yeah right,' I scoffed. 'Look, I'm in a hurry. What d'you want? Fancy meeting up tomorrow?'

'Nooo, that's what I phoned to saaay,' sang Frank.

'You sound really camp,' I said with delight.

The first time I had gone on holiday with Frank was at the end of my first year. RaviKavi weren't pleased. 'Haven't you made any nice friends at college? How can you go on holiday with a boy only? It's indecent. Why haven't you got any girlfriends, friends who are girls?' And I'd said triumphantly, 'Frank isn't a boy, he's gay, Mum.' 'Ufff,' my mother had said as though I'd let off a stink bomb in the front room, 'why do you have to talk about these things?' I had told RaviKavi they were out of touch with the modern world because there were lots of gay people these days, although I only knew Frank, but that wasn't the point. 'Yes, yes, thank you for informing us about the modern world,' said my father. It wasn't just a joke, they really hadn't wanted me to go, but they couldn't stop me now I was living away from home. I had got Frank to come and put in lots of dimmer switches for them as a consolation prize. 'He is a qualified electrician and he's also,' my mum lowered her voice, ... 'that thing.'

'I've met a great guy. I'm now officially taken, so you can't come over unannounced and spoil my credibility.'

'Great!' I laughed. 'We can go on a foursome. To the pictures.'

'You must be joking. Luke's too much competition.'

'Ha, ha. What's he like then?'

'He's a travel agent.'

I burst out laughing. 'What a surprise! I bet you had to go over the holiday in great detail together. Hope you got us a discount.'

'Naturally,' smirked Frank. 'Will Luke mind you going away for New Year?'

'No, we'll do Christmas in Brighton probably. It'll be fine.'

'You can't drop your friends just because you've got a boyfriend,' said Frank and I nodded at the phone. 'Anyway, I haven't got anyone else to go with.'

'You might have by then,' I said eagerly, although Frank's romances never lasted beyond the time it took to spell the guy's name.

'Then I'll drop you like a stone,' said Frank and we giggled. 'Where are you off to?'

'I thought you hadn't phoned to chat.'

'Just tell me then I'll go.'

'I'm going to a book launch, dah-ling.'

'Oooo. Verry poash. Who do you know who has book launches?'

'I know people,' I said mysteriously.

He laughed. 'OK, see you darling.'

I had a quick shower and walked about the bedroom wondering what to wear. I stared at my shalwar khameez sets inside plastic hangings from the dry cleaners, which had been there for months, because I only wore them to Indian occasions that I was forced to go to with RaviKavi. Amrit's book launch wasn't going to be an Indian event, even though I noticed it was in an Indian restaurant I'd never heard of, somewhere upmarket. It wouldn't be like the concerts at Brent Town Hall or the quawaalis and kavi sammelans at the Nehru Centre that I had been dragged to with RaviKavi. It wouldn't be Indian like that – disorganized and ostentatious saris and kids screaming and hands waggling and uncles shouting at the top of their voices. It would be English, sedate and elegant. I debated over it and then put on my usual black jacket over black trousers, and black T-shirt underneath with black boots. Frank was always telling me that I should stop wearing black because it was so unoriginal, but Luke wore black all the time as well and I wasn't sure of any colours that would suit me. I put on a bright red lipstick and Chanel 19 on my pulse points. *The Journey of One of Many* I repeated to myself on the bus as it pulled into town with lots of passengers. What did that mean?

CHAPTER THREE

I wanted to leave as soon as I got there. I didn't know what
had possessed me to come. The restaurant was full of people
in suits and women in skirt suits talking in huddles, and lots
of people stared at me when I walked in. At the last minute
I had put on my black velvet pillbox hat with a hatpin
through it, which I had worn for the last two years on
campus. I'd been known by it, it was my style, but here it
looked out of place, definitely not chic. Nobody asked to see
my invite although I had it ready in my clammy hand folded
into a fist inside my jacket next to my travel card. It was too
embarrassing to leave as soon as I'd come in, so I decided to
push through to the bar area, drink down one of the glasses
of champagne and then make a hasty getaway. I looked
around surreptitiously as I extended my hand to the tray of
cold glasses. Several old men in suits smiled encouragingly
at me and I drank down the glass quickly. The alcohol was
good and cold inside my neck and I boldly took another,
positioning myself against the bar as ballast. There weren't
many Indian people, a few men and only one woman, all
middle-aged and elegant. I couldn't see any weird people,

the weird people that Luke had said were part of Amrit's life. I was planning how I would relate the scene to Luke when I noticed Amrit through the crowd.

He was talking to a young woman with blonde hair which she was throwing over her shoulder as she laughed at something he was saying. I watched her disdainfully. She was one of those women who laughed in that girlish way when men made jokes. He was practised, I could see that. I knew next to nothing about him, but I knew he could make white women laugh. I knew they thought him clever and that made me despise him a little bit. Suddenly, he caught me looking through the bobbing heads, smiled and raised a hand in salaam, and went back to telling his jokes without missing a beat. I felt a surge of admiration for him because I thought he was clever at deceiving people. I put down my glass and walked out of the door.

It was a balmy evening, the sky still pale blue, the afternoon not yet finished with. I decided to walk down Dean Street into Shaftesbury Avenue and then on to Leicester Square. It was a circuitous route but there would be lights and strangers and bright restaurant windows and I was feeling a little foolish. As the warm air caressed my face I gazed at the pavements clumped with office workers chattering outside the pubs. I supposed at some stage I would be like them. I had a terrible feeling of exhaustion, my feet felt like lead and I wanted to get away from them and into the underground. I had just reached the corner of Shaftesbury Avenue, when I felt someone running to catch me up. I turned sharply, as alert as anyone walking alone in a city. It was Amrit, his hair a little dishevelled, his eyes shining.

'Bored already?' he said looking disappointed.

'No,' I shook my head, 'I just didn't really...feel very comfortable in there.'

'Neither did I,' said Amrit and grabbed my hand, pulling me across the road. 'Come on, I'm meeting some friends in the pub.'

I was shocked at his familiarity, but pleased at the way he

had involved me in a conspiracy. We entered a small dismal pub in Romilly Street. It must have been the only pub in London that summer which wasn't crowded and heaving. It was gloomy with faded pictures on the wall, little monuments to various Irish writers. Muffled gunfire sighs came from the fruit machines. I was surprised to see two old Indian men sitting at a little round table, their hands holding pint glasses. They didn't look very sophisticated, they were jowly and dressed in shabby tweed jackets.

'This is the Despair,' whispered Amrit in my ear and led me towards the table.

I shook hands with his friends and my eyes darted around the pub. It looked like a front room with lamps in corners and chintzy stools and begrudging fruit machines. This is the Despair, I was thinking, feeling bewildered by those words.

'Why don't you get them in?' suggested Amrit and pushed his wallet into my hand. The leather was warm, like a freshly-killed animal. I placed it on the bar and turned to look at the three men at the table engrossed in a conversation. I had a sudden urge to push the wallet into my face, inhale the musk, that vital precious part of the deer. Kastoori, that was the Hindi word for musk. What were those lines I'd heard one of the Visiting Gods recite once, lines from the great poet Kabir? The deer searches the whole forest for the musk, the scent he is so enthralled by. He searches and searches until he dies. And all the while, the musk is within him, inside his own belly button. As the pints arrived, making watery pools on the polished bar, I saw that the pub was called The Hope, and I felt strangely exhilarated, as though set free like a spring. And then Amrit was at my side.

'What are you doing in here with three decrepit old men?' he said as though he were admonishing me and I laughed out loud.

'I'm not with them, I'm with you.'

I was smiling broadly as I placed the drinks on the round table. One of his friends was saying that apparently Yeats went about not noticing anything for months and suddenly he would look out of the window and see something. He was so astonished that he thought he'd better write a poem about it. They all laughed uproariously. I watched their faces impatiently. That restlessness I had felt earlier in the day had returned, gaining momentum like an express train in my stomach. His friends must have felt it too, for they drank quickly and made their goodbyes.

I began lighting a cigarette with a book of matches. It was a trick I had learned from the Sunbeam. Using only one hand, you folded over the match, and rubbed it against the strike. The match would flare fantastically like a torch as you leant into the co-ool flame. Amrit was watching me curiously as I failed to complete the operation. Suddenly, he burst out laughing and offered me a light. I sucked on my cigarette shamefacedly.

'Want one?'

'Given them up,' he said without taking his eyes off my face.

'They kill you,' I said exhaling noisily.

'And are you intent upon killing yourself?' he asked with a raised eyebrow.

'Mmmm,' I said, jiggling about in the seat, sucking luxuriously on the cigarette, grinning at him. I felt in great command of myself, with the enormous ease that one feels at that point in life when one is busy acquiring new habits and ideas, rather than protecting and defending those already formed.

'What are you writing these days?' he asked politely.

'Well,' I frowned, 'I think I'd like to write a novel. About where I was born and all the people there, the families I used to know. My memories of childhood.'

'Mangoes and coconuts and grandmothers,' mocked Amrit. 'The Great Immigrant novel.'

'Oh,' I said and looked at him uncertainly, 'is it?'

'No,' he smiled. 'Go on.'

'It seems like a mammoth task, a lot of work and research,

I mean I'm not sure where you start but the competition made me feel that...' I noticed Amrit's eyes had wandered away from me, staring at the vacant seats his friends had left.

'Why do you talk to them?' I said abruptly. 'They're so old.'

'They remember things I remember,' he said, turning his attention back to me.

'Like what?'

He smiled. 'No Luke tonight?'

'We're not joined at the hip,' I retorted.

Amrit raised his eyebrows but didn't say anything.

'No, I don't mean that. I don't mean it in that way,' I said, shaking my head.

He was relaxed in his chair, his legs crossed, one finger on his cheek, his head tilted, listening.

'I owe so much to him. I wouldn't have seen the things and done the things. I wouldn't have learnt about. And he's so. But now.'

'He was your shield against the world,' said Amrit.

Yes, I thought, like RaviKavi, like everything, all the good strong things.

'And now it feels like a dependence,' said Amrit and smiled.

'That's exactly,' I said.

'How privileged we feel, in the présence of gods,' said Amrit and gestured around the pub with two fingers closed together, like a guide pointing out the monuments.

I looked up and saw the pictures, squinted to decipher the short texts below them. All at once I remembered being in India when I was sixteen or seventeen. RaviKavi had got it into their heads that along with my aunt and uncle we would all make a long journey, a circular route taking in one of the supposed trails that Raam had trudged, detailed in the Ramayana. It involved uncomfortable third-class train rides, early-morning tottering cycle rickshaws, reaching temples as dawn broke. The cacophony of darkness and chimes and wailing had sent me reeling outside to the light where I was caught in the sea of amassing devotees with garlands and upturned faces. None of my family had ever been religious. RaviKavi didn't have bronze gods sitting inside a corner of their larder in N3 like other Indians. It was the same story in India: at occasions like the first shaving of a baby's head, or the ritual before a marriage, my uncle's Brahmin servant had to be consulted on correct religious procedures; then the jokes would start about shortforming the rituals because dinner was ready.

I had been angry and irritated that they had involved me in this pilgrimage of heathens. I had sat grumpily outside, as the hordes washed along with flowers and unquestioning faith. My father had come out of the boisterous temple into the open, and explained that you didn't have to be a devotee. 'We are not religious,' he said, 'but we are god-fearing. It is necessary to be among gods at certain points in your life.' I peered at the pictures in the pub. Wilde and Swift, Yeats and Behan and Kavanagh. The usual suspects. The pub was deserted. They were waiting for us to leave.

'I'll get you a cab,' said Amrit.

I woke the next day in a violent state of agitation. I felt furious with myself. Snatches of the previous night's conversation spluttered around my head. I wondered if it had all been a dream or some kind of drug-induced madness. Had we really talked with such intimacy and for so long? Everything seemed intact in my bedroom and the sun was streaming insistently through the gaps in the curtains. I buried myself deeper under the duvet and made myself rational. After all, nothing had really happened, nothing I had to reproach myself for. I drew back the curtains and let the sun fall on my body and giggled. In a way, it had been quite exciting, in a drunken, crazy sort of way, the kind of thing I could make into an anecdote for Frank. The phone rang and as I padded into the front room I noticed how old-fashioned and ugly the flat looked with its cheesy magnolia walls and grey carpet. I reprimanded myself for not bothering to unpack the 'FRAGILE' wooden crates and cardboard boxes sitting around like Les Miserables.

'Mira,' shouted Luke, 'you'll never believe it. I've got the grant! The letter's been here for two days. Can you believe it?'

'That's great, Luke,' I said, stifling a yawn.

'You could sound more pleased,' he said stiffly.

'Oh Luke, it's brilliant. Honestly. Let's go out tonight and celebrate.'

'Great. Listen you know those beroccas, the vitamin B and magnesium tablets, the French ones? I can't find them anywhere.'

'I'll get them for you, you can't get them everywhere,' I said.

I had a sinking feeling as I put the phone down; there would be no way of evading the subject that Luke was bound to bring up tonight. I'd never dreamt that the Arts Council would actually hand over cash so easily for such an obscure project. I'd thought I was safe. In a spurt of activity I started pushing the boxes to the side of the room, and gave up almost immediately. I sat down on the floor and contemplated my legs in need of a wax. Amrit had stood in the street and smiled. He had given me the phone number of the university where he lectured. 'Come and have lunch some time, both of you,' he had said breezily and disappeared out into the night. I leapt up and started scrabbling around in my bag for the piece of paper. But I had lost it, it was nowhere. I felt a twisting of elation and panic in my stomach.

I walked around during the day, staring into shop windows and going in and out of Boots the Chemist, forgetting what I wanted to buy. I walked all the way to Hampstead, letting the sun toast my bare skin, skittering memories moving through my mind as I stopped off occasionally to have a coffee or look into the sumptuous shop windows. I felt as though I would soar up into the sky if I didn't keep walking and made a mental note to ask Tash about biorhythms, the next time she was in London. Perhaps she was in London, I thought suddenly, my heart jumping. It was like her to be around and not phone.

Tash was the person I'd known the longest after RaviKavi. She had come over to me on the first day of school and taken my hand. 'Hello, my name is Natasha Sayles.' Her dad had left when she was little, and her mum had gone out to work to support her and her sister. Her mum had strings of lovers who Tash would give generic names to: the Manic Depressive, the Fat Slob, the Dangerous Criminal. At the age of sixteen Tash had left school to become a traveller. Jobs in London were just a means to an end. Make some money and go. She made a point of being a traveller and not a tourist. She was always moving around, staying on floors. I hadn't seen her for a while, but she always wrote to me, never forgot my birthday. I realized I had always kept everybody separate, the university scene and the London scene, even my two best friends in London didn't know each other and had met Luke only a few times. I liked to keep people to myself. Frank said lone children didn't know how to share, they were selfish bastards.

The Burly Spaniard answered the phone, saying Tash was in London but not at home. I debated over leaving a message, because his English was no good. I'd see her soon. Our paths would cross naturally. I was planning to spend the rest of the summer letting things happen. I rather wanted to live spontaneously.

In the evening, when I got to the squat, the Sunbeam and the Oily Rag were sprawled around in the darkened front room watching TV, wedged between jungles of beer cans, giggling as they passed joints to each other. They said Luke was down the shops and to have a beer. They were watching a video, a habit that always struck me as outrageous in the early evening. The blue light in the room made everything look eerie and I ran upstairs into Luke's room to wait. I threw myself on the lumpy bed. Everything smelt of mould and cat litter. I could hear the cistern burbling in the 'organic' bathroom with its corn rows of green mould lining the tub. It was a huge Victorian house with its own peculiar language of creaks and groans and twangs in the night. I usually tried to avoid staying there. I curled up on the bed trying to read but the sentences swam past. I was thinking about the Despair and Amrit's head, tilted as he listened to me, the touch of his wallet in my hands.

My head hurt, and I scrunched up my eyes. A terrible hunch was pressing on my shoulders, a hunch that it was the best conversation I had had in years. The room was airless and humid. I knelt on the precarious bed and pushed my weight against the jamb of the sash window, fiddling and pummelling the latch, but it wouldn't give. I couldn't breathe. I pushed and pushed but it wouldn't budge until I fell away, exhausted with frustration and fury, thinking I was going to burst into tears. My heart was beating unnaturally fast and my breath was coming in bursts. I made myself be still for moments, before racing down the groaning stairs to the kitchen for a glass of water.

'Hi,' said Luke turning from the counter, an easy smile on his face. 'I was just getting us some beers.' He walked over and planted a wet kiss on my lips.

'How long have you been here?' I demanded. 'The bloody window's jammed again.'

'Yeah,' he said absent-mindedly, opening the fridge. It was packed to the brim with beer cans and cat food.

'It's such a dump this place,' I hissed, not that his flat-mates cared about my opinion even if they could hear me through the open door. The TV was on full blast, spewing out gunshots and car chases. I couldn't understand how, after living in the lovely house that Ralph and Matty had, Luke could bear this hovel.

'What's the matter?' said Luke, passing me a can.

'Nothing,' I said and took a huge gulp.

'Hey.' He chinked his can with mine.

'Oh yeah, congratulations,' I said unenthusiastically.

The cat, which they called Trenchtown, slithered its long-haired arrogance into the kitchen and made me jump. It was a scraggy ginger tom that one of them had adopted. All three of them spoilt it rotten and it hated girls, I was sure of it. I tried to kick it away, but it leapt towards Luke who scooped it up and smothered it with baby talk. It started purring disgustingly.

'How was the thing?' he said.

'Boring. How much did you get? I can't believe it. The Arts Council must be off their heads giving out cash left, right and centre,' I said.

'Five grand,' he smirked.

'What?' My mouth fell open.

The cat, knowing that attention had shifted from its ugly face for two seconds made a vicious hissing sound and shot out one of its flea-ridden legs at me.

'For god's sake!' I stepped back and the cat leapt out of Luke's arms and started running around the kitchen like a demented fool chasing its tail.

'He's just restless,' smiled Luke, "poor baby.'

'Why are English people so obsessed with animals?' I snapped.

'Hangover of a colonial past. What's the matter?'

'Nothing. Let's go to bed and watch TV.'

I buried myself inside the bedclothes as I watched him struggle with the window, the muscles of his back undulating, smooth like a well-oiled machine. After a couple of tries, he hiked the lower part open and was immediately drenched by a gust of rainy wind. I started to laugh and he turned round to me drippily. He looked like a puppy.

'Happy now,' he said, and slid in next to me.

'Ugh,' I protested good-naturedly, 'you're wet.'

He had lit an incense stick and two candles on the box next to the bed which served as a bedside table. There was an old black and white film on TV and the rain was dropping like diamonds on the window pane, reflected under the pale moonlight. Luke poured out two short glasses of Calvados that Ralph had given him for Christmas. 'Bliss,' he said, 'my girl, the rain and five grand.'

'Oh shit,' I said, 'I forgot the beroccas.'

'I forgive you,' he said and wiped rain off his eyebrow.

'Where shall we go?' I said, snuggling up. 'The Caribbean? Or maybe the States. I've always wanted to go to the States.'

'It's not for a holiday,' he said piously. 'Anyway it could be. You know where I want to go.'

I stared at the TV.

'Mira?'

'No, Luke.'

'Why not? I haven't got two heads or anything. I wouldn't be imposing. I'd just go and visit them, why not? We could go together. They must be missing you.'

'No way I'm leaving London this summer, what there's left of it. I want to be here. It's the first time in my life I can be alone and hanging out in London Town. I used to dream about being here by myself in the summer.'

'Great,' he said flatly.

'You know what I mean.'

'London stinks in the summer. It's full of tourists and crappy movies and sweat.'

'I like it,' I said stubbornly. 'The long evenings, people crowding together, mini skirts.'

'Are you ashamed of me? Is that what it is? Because I'm white?'

'Don't be stupid. Why are we discussing this?'

'I want to discuss it. You always avoid this subject. Why?'

I sighed heavily. I did owe him an explanation, there was no way out of it. I felt tired and aggrieved. 'It's complicated.'

'I'm listening.'

'Look, Luke, I don't know why you want to meet them anyway. They're just parents. It's just that I don't want you to meet them without...an introduction. I mean they've met Frank and known Tash for years, she's an old friend.'

'And I'm a new friend, so what?' he said, folding his arms across his chest.

'Look, if you turn up there, they'll start putting two and two together and come up with five hundred. And it won't just be them, it'll be aunts and uncles and neighbours and friends and the servant too. They'll start making up scenarios. Weddings and all that. You won't like it. You don't know what Indian people are like. They won't think we're just going together, they'll make a production out of it.'

RaviKavi wouldn't have been like that. They weren't like ordinary people. They were poets and they had all sorts of friends in India and they would have welcomed any friend of mine with open arms, become natural guides and hosts. True, they wouldn't have been able to resist making a joke with their friends about Luke's over-zealousness. Give him some water quick, before he faints, his eyelashes are white, what did he say, what did he say, they would snigger with their friends. Nam Ass Thayy!, very good, very sweet. Do it again, Ravi would say, pointing the video camera towards Luke – dutifully dressed up no doubt in full khaadi, the hand-spun, hand-woven cloth popularized by Gandhi. And the worst of it was, Luke would come back and say how friendly everyone had been, how welcoming, never suspecting how deep an Indian stare really goes. Tash and Frank had never made any concessions to RaviKavi or the 'Indian culture', never called them auntie and uncle, never learnt namaste, only ever inflicted their own Western mores of accepted politeness on to them. 'Hi, Kavita,' Frank would say cheekily and RaviKavi, at first bristling with humiliation, had learnt to accept it after a while. Oh, that Mira's friend, he's a funny character, he calls us by first names. It's in their culture, what to do? Still, I wasn't being fair to Luke and I knew it was something to do with wanting him at a distance. It wasn't the whole story and the realization of the whole story began to dawn on me as I spoke.

'You are ashamed of me. That's it, isn't it?'

'No, that's not it. I don't want the hassle of it. They'll build it up into some big number.'

'I thought we were a big number.'

'You know what I mean.'

'I hate that expression. It's so unexpressive.'

'Now you sound like Ralph,' I giggled.

Stony silence.

'I don't understand you sometimes,' he said slowly.

'Just leave it, Luke, there's nothing to understand. So you're definitely going to India then?'

'What is it you want, Mira?' he said, ignoring my plea for a normal conversation.

'Oh, Luke,' I sighed, 'I'm not like you. You know what you want to do, where you want to go in life, what position you want to hold. I don't know any of those things. We're opposite to the stereotypes. I'm supposed to be the hard-working achiever and you're supposed to be the slacker.' I laughed. Indian people of my parents' generation were always waggling index fingers towards the Arts and Sciences, proving how all the young Asian girls were leaving everybody behind. 'We're different, that's all.'

'I'm boring, you mean.'

'You're focused. I'm...disorientated. But I like it. I want to free float.'

'I thought you didn't like that sort of attitude. You're always having a go at the Sunbeam and the Rag, wasting their lives smoking dope.'

'There's a difference between wasting time and living intensely.'

Luke clicked his tongue.

'I know you think that's pathetic, that it's a sort of pose,' I sighed. 'Maybe it is. I don't care. I'm not lost. I'm not look-ing for my roots or trying to live something down. I just want to live.'

'Do you want to be with someone else?' he said in a small voice.

'No,' I said, shaking my head vehemently. 'No, that's not it.'

'Then what do you want?'

'I just want...I just want more. I don't know how to explain it. I'm bursting, sometimes I feel faint from the yearning of it.'

'I love you,' he said. 'That's intense enough for me.'

'That's not what I'm saying,' I said. 'I love you too,' I added, but it came out all wrong.

'Don't say it like that. Like an obligation. Don't say it at all,' he said and turned over. I watched his shoulders, the creamy skin against the flatness of the sheets. I could hear his breath rising and falling, awake to amends I could not make. All the good strong things, everything I'd known, I could feel it evaporating. Sometimes it feels like a dependence. Yes, that's exactly it. I placed my hand on his back and left it there till I drifted into sleep.

CHAPTER FOUR

The next day, Saturday, was Matty's birthday and Luke had borrowed the Sunbeam's car. It was typical of the three of them to live in a hovel, while owning flashy cars and motorbikes, exorbitant CD roms, and designer leathers. As well as the Calvados, Luke had posh German chocolates and organic soya milk. The plan was to get there early so we could change into our fresh clothes and help if any help was needed, although Matty ran a small upmarket catering service with a friend, so our early arrival was designed for pure courtesy. We were going to drive back in the evening. It wasn't a surprise party, because Matty didn't trust Ralph with the organization. I was looking forward to it and at the same time dreading the drive to Brighton. I suggested that he should give Matty the other print too, as they would make a nice pair and Luke said that if I didn't want it why didn't I just say. I said I thought it would be nice for Matty and we didn't talk of it again.

It was a beautiful car, lovingly restored since the seventies, and it had a fantastic name: The Sunbeam Rapier. It was pale blue with little fins in the back and dark-red leather upholstery. It took the road like a dream and according to the Sunbeam, needed a good run as it hadn't been out for a while. Luke's flatmates both had giggling stupid girlfriends who they paid less attention to than their cars and motorbikes.

It was yet another fine day and we took the road out of London easily, the tape playing as the sunshine sparkled against our eyelashes. The remains of last night ebbed away as the speedometer rose. I had woken from a fitful sleep wrapped in anxiety, unusual because sleeping next to Luke was never uncomfortable with duvets being pulled or feet getting cold. In the beginning days, Luke had sung a little song to me that he had been forced to learn at school and recite to the sniggering older boys, but now I associated it with our peaceful slumbers. He had been a pretty schoolboy and apparently at public schools this was a definite disadvantage. Pretty and fussy about his food. I was the first person he had told that he wasn't fussy, it was just that Ralph had forced him to eat turnips and spinach even after he'd thrown up. It was Ralph's idea of building character.

'Sing that song, Luke,' I said dreamily, lost in my memories. He knew exactly the one I meant.

> 'Come to me, soothing sleep.
> Come to me soothing slee-ep.
> And with thee bring.
> And with thee bring.
> Fo-ge-het-fulness and dreams.'

He sang in the high voice that always made me giggle. It could still send me off to sleep and I was planning on catching forty zeds before we got there. Conversation was at a minimum in any case and with the sun dappling my face I snoozed off. When I came to, refreshed and alert, I noticed we had made good time, we were almost halfway there. I opened the glove compartment rooting around for sweets, unwrapped one for Luke.

'You're a good driver. You should teach me to drive.'

'I love this drive, I always get a lump in my throat,' he said.

'Because you used to hate school,' I said, remembering how he had told me about being packed off at the age of seven.

'Yeah, not that home was much better but it's just the sea and the anticipation of it. Nostalgic, I suppose. But I never did this drive when I was young. Can you be nostalgic for an event which didn't happen?'

'Well, don't they say you can have a Race memory, so maybe you can have a parallel childhood memory too?'

'What's a Race memory?'

'Well, that you might not have been born in India or Africa for instance, but the memory of your ancestors lingers in your blood or something like that, engraved in a deep memory.'

'Makes sense,' he said.

'D'you think so? It sounds like nonsense to me. You can only remember what happened for real. All the rest is suggestion and fantasy.'

'Why d'you say it then?' he said crankily.

I sighed. 'Conversation, I guess.' And yet, I was already thinking that I had known Amrit once, somewhere between fact and fiction and myth.

Silence for a while. I rubbed the back of his neck in a shameless gesture of appeasement.

'How old were you when Ralph had his...when he left home?'

'Thirteen, just. Yeah, because he missed my birthday. He wasn't gone for long. He was back with his tail between his legs after a year.'

'Did you ever meet her?'

'No, but when I was older, when I was at uni, he suddenly got it into his head that he wanted to tell me all about it. I really didn't want to know, but he got all confessional.'

I giggled. 'Too much information Ralph.'

Luke laughed and I touched his shoulder.

'Amrit will probably be there, worse luck,' he said and a shot went through my veins.

'Why, how many people are coming?' I said, looking out of the window.

'About twenty.'

'So Ralph and Amrit go back a long way then?' I said conversationally.

'Amrit punched Ralph in the face, outside the Screen on the Hill.'

'What?'

'Apparently, so the story goes, Amrit had written his first novel and Ralph, who was working for the *Spectator* in those days, reviewed it. He totally trashed it. And Amrit went up to him in the cinema queue, total stranger, right, told him he was a philistine and punched his lights out. Later they became friends. I don't think he ever wrote a novel again.'

I laughed loudly at the story.

'He was around a bit when Ralph left, doing the consolation act with Mum.'

'I thought you said you didn't remember him.'

'Well, you know, I was away at school. He was around in the holidays. He did try to teach me chess. He's very good at chess.'

'Oh really?' I said archly. 'Why don't you like him?'

'I didn't say I didn't like him. I think he's a fake.'

'Meaning?'

Luke shrugged. 'He isn't serious about things. He doesn't take things seriously. He makes fun of people, himself, anything. He used to pretend he could read palms; the girls, my sisters would go mad for it. Matty too.'

I wondered if I should tell Luke about the Despair and decided against it. Nothing to tell. I didn't want to get into a discussion about it.

The house was a large white detached affair with curved roof tiles and leaded windows. It was set to the side of a huge cultivated garden with pathways leading to benches inside little alcoves bordered with clipped hedges. There was a flowering rockery full of yellow and violet blooms, and a collection of apple and plum trees. Some of the pathways meandered off into green darkness away from the house, the white pavestones turning to mossy blurs. A lot of people were already there, drinking and laughing around a long table set against the side of the house. We said 'Hi' and raced upstairs to change in the separate bathrooms, with floor to ceiling mirrors and thick plush wine-coloured carpets. It was exactly the kind of house that I used to wish RaviKavi could have made for me, and yet I could never imagine them living in a house that needed constant and diligent attention. It was from Luke that I had heard, at first disbelievingly, about the importance of wiping the basin first with a cloth and then with a paper towel to eliminate watermarks. RaviKavi would have died laughing, they'd never heard of such quaint English things like watermarks. I smoothed myself down self-consciously in the mirror, looking this way and that, wondering why I had made this choice.

Luke was already downstairs, talking to Matty at the foot of the stairs. He looked incredibly handsome, the crisp starched white shirt and the pale silk waistcoat which picked out the honey-coloured texture of his skin. His two sisters came flying through the door and flung themselves on him and he ruffled their hair and elbowed them good naturedly.

'Mira!' squealed Matty. 'You look so lovely. Is that silk?'

'Hi, Mira,' chorused the girls. Luke grinned at me, making a help! face as they dragged him off outside to make music selections. I reached over and gave Matty a peck on the cheek, observed myself in the hall mirror as we passed into the garden. The shalwar khameez was bright orange raw silk, fitted at the waist, with a panel at the front made up of blue, green and red embroidery around three misshaped circular mirrors. Mum had bought it for me last time from Haus Khas Village in Delhi, a real village which had been turned into a shoppers' paradise selling 'ethnic village designs' for well-heeled Indians. In keeping with what they called ethnic, everything was mismatched, so the shalwar was a tie dye of pale red and turquoise and the chunni flung over my shoulder was orange with gold thread. It was a little over the top, considering everyone else was wearing beige or Laura Ashley type gear, but I felt very feminine and pretty in it. And Indian.

I saw him straight away. He was helping himself to a drink, standing in a circle of five people. Luke and I were the only youngsters, apart from his two sisters who were teenagers. They had set up an ad hoc DJ system and were playing records from Ralph and Matty's collection of jazz music, the type without lyrics. I turned back inside, suddenly embarrassed, and scuttled into the kitchen to coo over the food extravaganza. The outside table was hosting canapes and Japanese crackers and olives stuffed with almonds and anchovies, but inside was the main event. There was a huge salmon, decorated with tiny opaque slices of cucumber for scales. Alongside were large bowls of salads, rustic bread and white butter and champagne on ice. I was staring at the eye of the salmon when Matty took my arm and led me outside. I felt the silk sticking to my underarm and everyone looked over at me appreciatively which made me feel even more shy. Then Luke was at my side and we started talking to some of his parents' boring friends who I couldn't remember. I didn't look over at Amrit and twenty minutes later he came over and shook Luke's hand.

'Congratulations!' he said. 'I hear you're all set.'

'I'll probably go next week. I've actually had all the jabs, it's just a question of the visa.'

'Next week?' I said in surprise looking at Luke.

Amrit just smiled and carried on talking. I looked away from them into the distance. He was talking about an American tour he was being forced to go on by his publishers and how it cut into precious writing time. I made myself stand erect in my high shoes and listen patiently, although I was dying to know when, where, what, how, but Luke was obviously not interested. As the conversation rolled on, I knew that Amrit wasn't going to mention the Despair, almost as if he knew that I hadn't, or was my imagination playing tricks with me? Ralph came along with glasses of champagne and we all toasted and drank the stuff down. I found myself inspecting Ralph's face, as though someone who had left his family for another woman would have tell-tale signs etched on his expressions. Luke pulled me away into one of the little alcoves, half hidden from the rest of the party.

'What do you mean next week, you're not serious?' I said.

'Don't you want me to go?'

'Well, why do you have to go so soon? It'll be boiling there. Why not go over Christmas?'

'No time like the present,' he said looking at me.

'How long are you going for?' I said miserably.

'I don't know. I want to go. I want to go straight away. Maybe it'll be good for us to have a break.'

'This is about last night. You're crazy. Take my mum and dad's address. Do what you want. I'll give it to you.' I said angrily.

'Let's not fight,' he said. 'We'll talk about it later.'

Everyone sat around the house, inside and out, eating from bone-china plates balanced on their knees draped with soft napkins. More people had arrived, it was a throng, interspersed with a gaggle of teenagers who seemed to have appeared out of nowhere. From the edge of the garden you could see the misty dome of the Pavilion wreathed in clouds. The sky was turning a pale lavender. I walked away from the house, letting my heels sink heavily into the rich earth, walking slowly and methodically, watching my feet. A set of size tens came into view and I looked up sharply.

'Hello again,' I smiled.

'You look beautiful,' said Amrit. 'Why are you here alone and looking so sad? Because your boyfriend is playing a silly game with you?'

'He's not playing a game,' I said and then smiled. 'Just felt like a walk.'

'Shall I leave you?' he asked chivalrously.

I opened my mouth to speak and he put a finger on the

side of my lips as if to wipe something away. I gasped. My hand flew to his and my eyelids flickered. I could hear the distant chatter and clinking of glasses but it felt very far away. His eyes were staring into mine.

'I just wanted to touch you,' he said softly and removed his hand.

'We'd better go back,' I said evenly.

'Indeed,' he said, his face expressionless again.

We were met halfway by Matty and another couple who asked Amrit what his opinion was on some book the *Sunday Times* had been praising, a novel about the pornography industry, written by an ex-prostitute. The Sundays were claiming the author as the next important feminist icon. Matty and the others listened intently when Amrit said that these days victimhood was in vogue, either it was black or female or working class. He said that literature was being written by barbarians, it had become a cheap and shameless public relations racket. I don't remember what they said, it was a blur to me. I stood next to the group, feeling myself sinking slowly into the mud. Then suddenly a phone rang and everybody started looking around. Amrit produced his mobile with an apologetic grimace. My ears pricked up.

'Yes. Yes. I thought you'd organized it. Oh. Well. No not really. Alright. I said OK. Give me half an hour.' He flipped off the phone and everybody else had started talking amongst themselves. He walked a little further away and punched the keypad. He was speaking so softly that I couldn't hear a word. I'd always wanted to be able to do that. It was a trick you learnt in offices.

'Ahh,' he said, coming back into the group, 'I'm sorry. I have to be somewhere. My apologies, Matty.'

'Ohh no,' said Matty, visibly crushed. 'Trouble?'

He sighed. 'When is there no trouble? I thought it was all arranged, but there's been a hitch with the violin classes.' He laughed jovially as though he'd told a joke.

'I am needed apparently,' he said wryly and smiled at the party.

I noticed some of the faces seemed to be looking sideways or smiling politely. Matty was pursing her lips sympathetically. I blinked uncomprehendingly. It sounded like something important, yet he was being so casual about it and somehow his lack of urgency impressed me. Amrit laughed and said something which made my head jerk around to catch him smiling. A phrase in Urdu, which I assumed to be a part of a poem or gazal, because he said it in an over-exaggerated tone of grave longing. 'Who is there, who is not in need!' he recited and giggled when he saw my eyebrows flying like trapdoors.

It seemed to confuse or mystify the others and this reaction served to amuse him. He offered no translation, and I was inexplicably embarrassed, understood that I was supposed to understand. But understand what? In any case, there was a polite silence and then rapid heartfelt goodbyes. He didn't say any special goodbye to me and I watched him swaggering off down the lane. Men of his age didn't generally swagger, but then Amrit didn't seem to be a number of things I had imagined him to be. I made my way hurriedly into the house on the pretext of going to the loo, because I was afraid someone would say something. But say what? The phrase he had used wasn't dirty or rude, but the meaning was untranslatable. The depth of feeling inappropriate as a response to a phone call.

As evening fell and many of the guests began to drift away, to snooze or sit in the drawing room, Luke and I went to say goodbye to Matty who was sitting next to Ralph on one of the large white sofas. He had flung his arm around her shoulders. I stared at them for a moment and wondered how all had been forgiven. I couldn't imagine RaviKavi ever forgiving each other for such a heinous crime, but then again, I could never imagine either of them having the time or inclination to find another person to hold the interminable conversations they had with each other, about everything under the sun. And Ravi made Kavita laugh out loud, with some of his outlandish schemes – making a pilgrimage around religious sites in their forties for one, saving the black seeds from watermelons, drying them on newspaper and patiently spending all evening cracking open the kernels for another. But happiness and contentment were individual; who was I to say that Ralph and Matty weren't happy? Luke and I must have looked happy and we were, weren't we?

'I haven't had a chance to talk to you at all,' said Matty and shifted up to make room for me. I felt a deep need to comfort her, or at least to let her know how much I liked her. When I'd first met him, Luke had smiled at my assessment of people, the categories I had in my head of good and bad people. It was a distilled legacy from RaviKavi again, and although I would argue with them – what do you mean she's from a good family, who is good, what are your criteria for good? – I knew nevertheless. To be good and decent was to be kind and generous and proper. Matty, and up till now Ralph too, had fallen in this category for me. And Luke by association of course. With all these good and decent people in my life as sandbags, I was stoutly determined to be as bad as I could.

As I sat and talked about something to Matty, watching her carefully made-up face, I had a sudden feeling of terror that everything I knew was wrong, that people were monsters, not gods. Terror, because I was startled that it had taken me twenty-four years to realize things that most people knew off by heart like the alphabet.

'... come and see us, just because Luke's not around,' she was saying.

'Sure, of course.' I was embarrassed because neither of them was making a point about me not going with Luke to India, which after all was my home, or one of my homes. I was very very glad of the English stiff upper lip, because I knew they wouldn't dare to have questioned Luke over the matter. English parents had a fantastic regard for the privacy of their children, an attitude I found as exciting as my first taste of mangoes in season. Ralph wanted to show Luke a chair he had bought in the auction, and they headed out of the room to Ralph's study. I watched Matty's faint smile lighting up her face.

'Why do men only come close when they are going to be parted?' she said with a frown. I squeezed her hand. I could see she was proud that they were making an effort.

'Men are from Mars, women are from Venus?' I suggested with a grin.

'You know I read a whole slew of those American type books once. Women who love too much, the Cinderella complex. They're terribly depressing. I think women should be encouraged to have more adventures, don't you?'

'Men too,' I said.

'Yes,' she said searching my face. 'Yes, I suppose that's what Luke's doing. Trying his wings out. Oh,' she smiled suddenly, a sad smile, 'I mean in his work. He's very much in love with you, you know?'

'Matty!' I said, colouring slightly.

'You know,' she said, suddenly lowering her voice, 'I had a little adventure once. When Ralph was...buggering about.'

I was shocked at her phrase, at how lightly she put it and embarrassed that she assumed I knew about her private life. RaviKavi had instilled in me this practice of not discussing family details with outsiders. It was an unwritten law of the Indian constitution as far as I was concerned. One did not discuss what was within these walls, whether it was to do with money or love. Obviously, I was delirious when I realized that middle-class English people thought nothing of discussing their most intimate details, called their mum and dad by their first names and, most horrifically and deliciously, wandered about the house in the nuddy! When Luke told me this was common practice in their house I had screamed with disgust. I had never really got the hang of him hovering about in the bathroom while I sat on the toilet. RaviKavi had managed to endure twenty-eight years of friendship and marriage without getting that close. In our house, the bathroom had been a place of privacy, where you read books, smoked and came up with brilliant ideas.

'Matty!' I said in mock horror.

She giggled and then her face seemed to cloud over. 'I went away for a dirty weekend with a man,' she said. 'Funny, isn't it? Most people come to the sea for that sort of thing, but we went to a hotel in the heart of London.'

I couldn't hide my utter admiration at her gall.

'They wouldn't allow smoking in the room and he kept getting up in the night to go to the car. It was quite funny really. He smoked so much.' Her face looked sad, like the face of someone to whom another's well-being is terribly important.

'What happened?' I whispered conspiratorially.

'Oh it was all rather sordid. Trying to get back at Ralph, I suppose. I didn't really know what I was doing. Trying to prove I was a child of the sixties.' She laughed a high-pitched laugh.

'Didn't it last?' I said with concern.

'He disappeared,' she said and waved her hand. 'He bought me a rather nice scarf from Liberty's. That was nice.'

Then Ralph and Luke were back and her expression changed. I felt my skin crawl with embarrassment at the strange pathetic confession. A scarf! It sounded like some kind of apologetic payment a man had made to an incompetent mistress.

'Why don't we have lunch when you're next in town?' I said suddenly. 'You do come to London sometimes?'

Matty beamed at me. 'I'll certainly take you up on that,' she said.

In the car, Luke was smiling. 'You're good at families,' he said.

'Please,' I said, imitating Frank's Jewish shoulder hunch, 'I'm Indian.'

Frank had got his name from his mother's devotion to Sinatra. His parents were what he called Embarrassed Jews, who had shortened their name to Marks and moved out of

Golders Green. One day Frank had woken up and turned Jewish with a capital OY. He had reverted to his full surname and started celebrating festivals just to piss them off.

'Yeah, I think I did notice that,' said Luke lightly.

We laughed, enjoying the breeze rolling in through the windows. The tape was playing and I felt that nice feeling of having had just a little too much to drink and eat, feeling squiffy, unperturbed, floating.

'You're really going, aren't you?' I said.

'And you really don't mind, do you?' he said, and because I was caught up in something, some feeling of well-being, I didn't understand that it was an accusation.

'No,' I said simply, 'I really don't.' I didn't have the feeling of being wrenched away from him, didn't feel the need to make him stay, even wanted him to go and experience the world and let me be to experience the sun. This is a feeling of freedom, I thought, to be engaged and detached, which was the instruction that Lord Krishna gave to Arjun in the verses of the Bhagwat Gita. Arjun is on the battlefield, his armies behind him, when he realizes that the opposing army is made up of his brothers. He becomes immobile, doesn't know what to do. Lord Krishna, his charioteer, instructs him. He tells him that he must act, he must do what he has been placed on earth to do. He must fulfil his destiny. He must engage in battle, for he is a warrior and, knowing the facts, he must remain detached from his emotional ego.

So hang on, auntie, does that mean that Saddam Hussein, Hitler, can be justified? No, no, beti, Hinduism is about metaphor, allegory, ways of being.

I was watching the vanishing point hazing and receeding in front as the road flowed. Suddenly, the tarmac started flying, speeding past my eyes at a horrific speed. The interior of the car rattled as the road kept coming. My heart leapt in horror.

CHAPTER FIVE

The speedometer had climbed to ninety and Luke's foot was pressed to the accelerator. I stared at him, his eyes were transfixed to the road, his jaw set.

'Luke!' I screamed. 'Are you trying to kill us or what?'

Within moments, he had the car under control and we were driving fast but not dangerously. My heart was beating like a drum and my skin shuddering with relief and bewilderment.

'I thought you wanted to live intensely,' he said and smiled in a way I had never seen him smile. It wasn't the kind of smile that fitted with his face; it was snide and mis-shapen.

'Pull over on the shoulder,' I said tightly.

Silently, he pulled the car over. I got out, my legs trembling and when he came around the side and was standing beside me, I slapped him so hard across the face, that he was thrown against the car door. We stared at each other and his smarting face looked so vulnerable and sad that we suddenly fell into a hug, closed our arms around each other. It was the embrace of friends, not lovers, I knew.

'I'm sorry,' he said, 'I'm really sorry. It was calculated, I mean I had the car under control. But still. It was stupid.'

Watching his serious face made me smile. I started giggling and he started giggling too. The risk he had taken, the ridiculous, pointless, uncharacteristic risk to prove a point, struck both of us as ludicrous.

'Faaaark,' he said, extracting two hunched cigarettes from his pocket. We leant against the car and smoked for a while, our backs to the road.

'Faaark, if we hadn't died, the Sunbeam would have killed us.'

We laughed hysterically, choking on our cigarettes.

'It's OK,' he said, rubbing my back. 'It's OK.'

I looked at him. 'You know...'

'You're my best friend. That's a historical fact. That's all that matters. Will you help me pack?'

'We're officially breaking up?' I said, pulling back my lips from my teeth.

'On the count of three,' he said and smiled.

When we'd got together, on that dark uncomplicated night at the harbour, stared at each other, kissed endlessly, felt a series of emotions, wondered about the future, felt blessed, I had asked him if we were now officially going out together. He'd said yes, on the count of three.

'Luke,' I said, suddenly grabbing his hand. Out of the corner of my eye I saw cars flying past. 'Luke, I'm scared.'

He put his arms around me and squeezed. 'We'll be alright. You and me.'

The next week passed quickly. Luke was busy with packing and plans and seeing people and I ticked off things on the list.

Leatherman knife
Thermos flask
Sink plug
Insurance

Torch
Hat
Electric element to boil water with
Toilet rolls
Water purification tablets.

I stared at the list in bewilderment. What do you need all that stuff for, you're not going to the Bush on manoeuvres, I was about to say, but I kept my mouth shut. It was a bit like looking in someone's shopping trolley in the supermarket, guessing what kind of lifestyle they led. I was fascinated by the complete lack of overlap in my family's luggage (which was usually crammed with useless presents for relations and friends) and Luke's luggage. And why was it we never took out an armful of medical insurance, or ten rolls of Kodak or sun hats? I had never thought you needed so much to survive in India, it had never occurred to me. And unlike us, filling the suitcases with clothes for every occasion, Luke packed a smattering of T-shirts and shorts in his rucksack.

It was relatively painless. Neither of us talked about it, we hugged each other and even slept with each other on nights when it was inconvenient to go back to our respective homes. It was like a countdown and although we didn't say so, I'm sure we were congratulating ourselves for being so adult and civilized. We'd see each other after six months and talk of our adventures. We didn't discuss the possibility of meeting other people, because in our heart of hearts we didn't believe it, thought that the separation was some kind of obscure test, not of friendship, but of passion, of the possibility of a future.

On his last night I arrived at the squat with a bottle of Cava to find the house suspended in a strange atmosphere. The TV was turned down and the Sunbeam and the Oily Rag were reading newspapers. I was surprised to see them all at home as they had planned on playing pool till closing time. I padded into the kitchen to find Luke standing at the window, with his hand holding the grimy net curtain away from the pane.

'Luke?' I said.

He turned round. His eyes were red and he looked tired.

'You OK?' I said moving towards him.

He sucked in his lips and nodded. We kissed. I heard him swallow and the words seemed to be laden with effort. 'That's great. Shall we open it? The boys can have a glass too.'

'Sure but?' I looked at him quizzically and then squeezed his hand. I didn't know what to say. We'd managed the break up so well so far and I couldn't bear to see Luke crying or anything like that. I decided to be bright and cheerful.

'Right, where's a teatowel?' I started searching around the kitchen drawers. Thankfully the nasty little cat hadn't shown its ugly face around. It was probably sleeping away its fat little life as usual. I popped the cork and poured out the bubbly into two glasses and two mugs. I carried the mugs into the front room and smiled at the lads. 'Blimey,' I chortled, 'it's like a wake in here. Luke's coming back, you know. I never knew you all cared so much. Ahh.'

'It's Trenchtown,' said the Oily Rag quietly.

'Where?' I said spinning around, but nobody laughed as they always did at my unreasonable dislike of the animal.

'He got run over this afternoon,' said the Sunbeam.

I ran into the kitchen and finding it empty, raced upstairs, taking the steps two at a time. I threw open the door of Luke's room. It was pristine with the rucksack neatly laced up in a corner. He was sitting on the bed looking out of the window, the two glasses left untouched on the bedside boxes.

'Oh baby,' I said, hugging his head into my chest, 'why didn't you tell me about the cat? I'm so sorry. So sorry.'

'Stupid, isn't it?' said Luke, his face crumpled. 'It was just a cat. Scraggy old thing.'

'No he wasn't. He was your friend. You cared for him.'

'I just thought he would always be safe. You know? I mean he was fat and lazy and he was happy to just sit about the place. He didn't even bother going out very often, didn't even get into fights with the local mogs. And then out of the blue, he got some idea into his head to go into the street. I mean, what sort of decision was that?' Luke laughed. 'Listen to me. I'm talking about a cat. I'll be alright.'

We went to sleep that night and although my eyes were closed, I wondered if Luke was having the same thoughts. I had a feeling the death of the cat represented something to him, and you didn't need to be a psychoanalyst to work that out. I thought it better to leave well alone. The cat was dead.

Luke didn't want Matty and Ralph at the airport, so Frank had offered to take us in his 'flashy drug-dealer car' as Luke called it. It had a collapsible roof and unnecessary bull bars at the front.

'Vitara! Vitara!' snapped Frank at me. 'Not Victoria! My car's no cissie. Tell her, Luke. God she knows nothing.'

'She's only interested in the colour,' said Luke.

'Is it blaaaak?' they both chorused together.

At Terminal 3 Frank shook Luke's hand and then hugged him. They liked each other immensely, my best pal and my best pal, and Frank said Luke was one of the few straight men who didn't balk at being hugged in public by another man. A big compliment from Frank. Then he walked off so we could say goodbye. I swallowed as I stared at him with his rucksack and jaunty kerchief round his neck. He was smiling at me broadly.

'Take care of yourself,' I said and handed him RaviKavi's address. 'Phone them if you get into any trouble. Or if you're in the area.'

I meant it. It was different now, I wasn't threatened by his presence in their home, no longer suspicious that he would turn up and foolishly ask for my hand in marriage. I knew he wouldn't contact them at all. I couldn't help thinking of the time, only some seven months ago when I had waved RaviKavi off in the same airport and how excited I had felt to be free of obligation and dependence.

In the car driving back home Frank asked me how I felt and I felt fine. It was only in the following days that a strange panic began to set in. Suddenly, with my empty days stretching ahead of me, freedom threatened to turn into void. I stared at the flat with its crates and cardboard boxes. It was as though my previous skin was lying in tatters around me, still attached, while this new skin that I had been so looking forward to, hadn't formed yet. It was still raw and fragile. I felt I must do something, but what?

While Luke was around, I had been happy to while away the days sitting in the sunshine, letting London wash over me, but the weather had entered a phase that the weathermen called 'changeable'. Although it was the tail end of August and there had been stretches of sunny days and long warm nights turning the capital into a sticky Mediterranean city, now suddenly it was one day rain, the next day cold and the next day sun. It was confusing, you didn't know what to wear, felt compelled to have that English conversation about the weather, had to walk the street resignedly with an umbrella, just in case.

The grey skies seemed to be taunting me and I felt an urgency to act. I found myself in a bookshop looking for Amrit's book but it was nowhere to be found and I left the shop feeling slightly ashamed. I didn't think there would be an opportunity for us to meet again and I wasn't sure I wanted it either. I remembered sinking into the mud as he was answering his mobile telephone, remembered his fingertip on my face and I had the feeling I wasn't ready for freedoms that I could not name.

On a day full of that peculiar chill in the air that heralds the end of summer, Tash appeared in my life like a parachute. She had been doing the slew of music festivals around England, running a 'chai' stall and selling incense sticks with a group of NFA people like her. No Fixed Abode meant it was difficult to get money out of the SS and automatically deemed you outside the confines of regular society. With the summer festivities over, she had tried to return to her mother who was living with the Burly Spaniard. He was learning English by playing Scrabble and would upturn the board periodically when Tash pointed out a word he had made up. Tash had left, slamming the door. She needed a place to crash for a few weeks and I was delighted to have a flatmate.

The leaves were still green when she moved in with her meagre luggage and multicoloured bags. She was wearing her usual American army trousers with two way zips, and a white vest under a baggy black army shirt. She'd chopped off all her hair and from behind she could be mistaken for a boy. At school she had been the first girl to possess breasts. In classes she used to wear tight blouses that showed off her magnificent cleavage and even male teachers had been seen to blush. She had left school and travelled around the world and learnt things about herself and now she put all that infantile behaviour down to wanting to get her estranged father's attention.

She had been living on her wits for years, swinging back and forth between continents, freewheeling between homes. I was impressed by how little she needed to survive and how well she adapted to the space allocated to her. Although I told her it didn't matter, every morning when I came to the kitchen, she had already put back the sofabed into a sofa, straightened up the cushions and cleared up the debris from last night. She began to transform the flat.

She approached the task with a military precision I had never known in RaviKavi's chaotic existence. Over a weekend, she ripped out the carpet and sanded down the floorboards. Then she moved all the crates to the sides of the room and began to find places for the things inside. She put up a series of shelves and lined up the books and candlesticks in order. She washed, ironed and hung up the blue curtains I had lugged back from India and stuffed in a suitcase. She ran up cushion covers in an afternoon from velvet and silk garments purchased from the Oxfam shop and arranged all the half-finished lotions and potions in the bathroom cabinet. Outside the flats was a place where the range of council refuse bins were kept. Propped up next to the bins were items too large to fit. Three large cardboard boxes, a wardrobe door, a shopping trolley with a broken toaster inside. 'Perfect,' she announced, hauling the wardrobe door into the flat. Upturning it to reveal its veneered grain, she placed it across the two crates marked Fragile, to make a desk facing the trees. She even left the brass door knob on underneath; as she said, it was at the perfect angle for me to play with when I was working out chapters!

The flat was evolving into a living space, a place of home. There was still no coffee table and we sat on the floor to eat our dinner and lunch. Some nights I had to turn on the heating and we held our steaming bowls of chocolate with both hands like they did in French movies, watching the leaves outside the window dwindling towards the earth.

One night, we decided to go to a Tarot reading in one of the shops in Covent Garden. The fraudulent old woman made us laugh. She looked like she was wearing a wig and her nails were like claws. At the last minute, Tash bottled out, said she didn't want to know the future. I was hungry for mine. As I watched the woman laying out the cards, concentrating on them, I felt a little bewitched, convinced my future lay in the hands of a stranger. I picked out the cards excitedly, making a big fuss over the ones I picked, as though she were doing a magic trick and I wanted to confound her. She smiled patiently as I shuffled and reshuffled the cards, determined to mix them all up, break any patterns or trickery she might have up her sleeve. She started to lay them out as I ogled the beautifully exotic images. The Queen of Cups, the King of Swords, Death upside down, the Sun.

I faintly remembered RaviKavi forbidding me to go to any quacks and charletons as they called them, when on my first trip back home I had insisted on having my palm read, wanted my future on a plate. They had even mislaid the kundli, the horoscope made for every Indian child at its birth, a prediction of its future. RaviKavi didn't believe in all that sort of stuff; they said my destiny was going to be designed by me.

'I can see a man,' said the woman, and I grinned. 'He's dark.'

'Tall, dark and handsome,' I said encouragingly. It wasn't Luke then, I told myself excitedly.

'Tsk, tsk, tsk,' went the woman and I peered at the cards eagerly.

'So many swords. Are you sure you shuffled properly?'

Tash kicked me under the table and I hid a smirk.

'There is a lot of suffering. I see death.'

I frowned. I thought they weren't supposed to see death. She smiled.

'Ahhh, yes. Another man. And another. Yes I can see it now. It is Arthur and his Knights. They are sitting at the Round Table. War has devastated everything, smoke everywhere, but in the far distance there's a new country with glistening spires and turrets. They can't see, they're slumped around the table. They're all wearing armour. It's rusting. They've been sitting there for years, even they don't know how long.'

'De-de-de-de-de-de-de-de,' Tash hummed the theme tune to *The Twilight Zone* in my ear.

'And there you are,' said the old witch.

'Who, me?' I said innocently.

'You're a warrior too. You're shaking one of them. His armour's very rusty. Oh, he's dead. Then you try another, he's dead too. You're looking for the one who matters, the one you have been to all the expeditions with, that one, your companion. You've got him, you start shaking him. Shaking him and shaking him. You've got to go to the new country ahead, that's what you have to do. Part of the job description for a warrior is to keep exploring. But you don't want to go alone. Bits of his armour fall off, the rust is melting it away. You keep shaking him. You're shouting, "You're alive, you're alive. Wake up. You're alive."' She was speaking rapidly as though in a trance. Suddenly she jerked her head.

Tash and I were shrinking away from her, our eyes like saucers, both considering how we could make a dash for the door, before this nut got any nuttier.

'It's no good,' she said earnestly. 'He's dead, you see,' and fell into a slumped silence.

'Right anyway thanks,' said Tash grabbing her coat and bag.

'What did I say just now?' said the old woman in confusion.

'Ummm. Nothing much relevant. Doesn't matter,' I said smiling.

'Ahem,' she said, peering at the cards on the table as if they were sawn-off shotguns. 'Yes, I can see a journey. A journey that must be made.'

'A journey straight back to that nuthouse, darling,' hissed Tash.

'There is light, yes, I see light at the end of the journey. There's fortune and fame. This card,' she said, picking up a card and waving it frantically under my nose.

'What does it mean?' I said excitedly.

'Change,' she said. 'Irrevocable change.'

I smiled. Exactly. But how, when, where and why?

'Sometimes these things can be projections,' explained the woman. 'Perhaps I'm not in the right frame of mind for it. You see, it could be about me or her, not you. That happens sometimes. These are not a young person's cards.'

'Huh?' All our futures confused together in my cards. Surely that wasn't allowed, there must be a mix up in the administration. I chuckled, thinking that it must be an Indian administration, full of head lolling clerks sending you from pillar to post, giving out misinformation.

'Complete waste of money,' said Tash, linking her arm through mine. The next day she received a phone call from her sister.

'My mum's sick,' she said. We stared at each other

incredulously. Her mum, the gritty career woman who had strings of lovers, had been diagnosed with a cancerous lump in her breast. I was shocked and afraid for Tash. These kinds of crises weren't supposed to happen till you were old, thirty at least. She declared she was going home. She said she would make it up with the Burly Spaniard. She felt compelled to be near her mum. For the first time since I had known her she seemed wrapped up in thoughts that I could not imagine or infiltrate. I didn't know what to do. She spoke cryptically, her sentences annotated with silences. I knew it was the talk of death which had startled her but we didn't speak about it, we didn't know how. She packed up all her belongings, her face wan. I saw her looking at the telephone warily, as though it could go off any minute. I put my arm around her and wondered what was going through her mind that night as she lay stranded on the sofabed. In the morning she seemed to be doing everything in slow motion.

'Everything will be alright,' I said. 'Phone me.'

She nodded and walked towards the train, stooping a little. She seemed older from behind. I watched the train disappear in the distance. As I stood amongst the scurrying commuters in the middle of the concourse of Victoria Station, a million memories swooped down on me like a flight of crows. Deafening overlapping voices and cries and anecdotes and layer upon layer of superimposed images. Like a schizophrenic confused in the community, I crept homeward, without saying a word to a soul. I returned to the quiet gentleness of my flat. Without eating anything, I sat down at the makeshift table made from raw materials and I began to write.

CHAPTER SIX

Day and night, I sat huddled over the computer, my fingers flying across the keys. I had no plan or design, just a powerful urge to remember, grab all the memories swirling around my head. The things that needed to be done I did dutifully and methodically: checking RaviKavi's house for break-ins and politely chatting to their next door neighbours who had a spare key, making sure I didn't exceed the spending of RaviKavi's carefully calculated allowance, indulging in short frantic telephone calls with Frank who regaled me with details of his latest romantic entanglement, eating, cooking, washing myself. All the tasks of ordinary existence became a backdrop to my work. Memories I thought I had forgotten or deemed irrelevant, came back to me vividly, suddenly precious gems of my life. I felt myself in a kind of trance, as though I was seeing a movie in my head and writing down what I saw, as quickly as I could. Wide shot: our little family leaving the MRI colony for London, and the shoals of neighbours coming to Santa Cruz airport with garlands. Close up: eating bhelpoori and drinking kala khatta (black sour sherbet) on Juhu beach, watching the dancing monkeys dressed in skirts and ankle bells. I smiled wryly when I found myself writing about the first Alphonso mangoes in Crawford Market; cool green coconuts cracked open by men with sharp knives; my grandmother falling asleep in the cinema hall and insisting she hadn't lost the plot. The Great Immigrant novel, Amrit had mocked.

RaviKavi phoned at weekly intervals and sent blue aerogrammes full of news and views. They wanted to be sure that I was managing and I told them I was surrounded by friends. It was true, because in some strange way, I had recalled everybody who had existed in my past. All the people I had known and all the conversations I had heard became my friends and accomplices; I felt myself watched over by the silent witnesses in my room, the little ornaments and candlesticks that Tash had arranged so lovingly. When my mind was exhausted, I turned and twisted the brass door knob, so conveniently situated by my right hand. Opening the door, as Tash would have smirked, to new ideas.

I watched the little dots making up the letters making up the words appearing on the computer screen, one after the other. I kept printing them out to make sure they were real. I felt I was in the middle of some elaborate task of creation, piecing together all the hundreds of fragments of a vast jigsaw. Sometimes I would wake in the middle of the night, jumpy with dreams of that gone-for-ever scraggy cat which I had looked upon with such suspicion and annoyance. I didn't want to think of it. I forced myself to get out of bed and write some more, remember details about the childish days. After a while I understood that I must be writing some kind of novel, because it had grown too long to be a short story.

Sometimes I found myself laughing at my jokes and crying at some slight that a fictional character made to another, and at those times, claustrophobic with voices, I would take a walk in the woods behind the flats, staring at the red and orange leaves, feeling the delicious smart of the breeze laced with bonfires. I felt enormously powerful, oozing with energy and momentum, taking long purposeful strides, cracking my knuckles as I marched along the spongy grass. From time to time I remembered my encounter with Amrit in the Despair and felt that it, like the other events in my recent past, had an enormous significance, a significance which was obscured. But it was lying in wait for me, like an accident waiting to happen.

Matty phoned me one day in the middle of November and said she'd like to take me for lunch. We met in Hampstead and ordered the *prix-fixe*. I suddenly had no idea why I was meeting her, the mother of my ex-boyfriend. I couldn't think of anything to say when she gave me short sketches of Luke's progress with his research. In fact she seemed to think I would have information for her, and I felt embarrassed because I couldn't furnish her with the comfort she needed. I had received just one postcard which sounded happy and eager. I remembered how I had felt sorry for her and it struck me as monstrous to have felt sorry for someone in their house, on their birthday, when they should have been at their most safe, intact and powerful. I wondered if that was how Ralph had felt when he came back with his tail between his legs. I couldn't bring myself to tell her I was writing.

'How's Ralph?' I asked.

'Oh, he's always buggering about somewhere,' she said tightly. 'I wish Luke would write more often.'

I shrank from the intense feeling of pity I felt for her, because I was not used to that feeling in connection with a grown-up person; it frightened and appalled me. When you were pitied, you had reached the end of your self respect and identity. I couldn't bring myself to like somebody I felt sorry for, because it made us unequal in a horrendous way.

'Do you see Amrit very often?' I asked casually, partly to change the subject and partly because I found myself wondering at his enigmatic departure from the party.

'Now and then,' she said quietly and rotated the spoon in her coffee cup. She smiled slightly. 'I thought perhaps you might have bumped into him.'

'Me? No, no.' I shrugged. 'Why, does he live in North London?'

'He lives in several places,' she said. She looked at me and quickly looked away. I had an odd feeling that I had got the lunch all wrong, that in fact she wanted to know if I had any dealings with Amrit, and had used the guise of concern over Luke to get my audience, and now she was embarrassed about it. It was a fantastic idea and I allowed it no further leverage. If you let your mind freewheel, you could imagine all kinds of strange things. Although we kissed goodbye with promises, I knew I wouldn't see her again and in some way I felt relieved. I was eager to return to my work, eager to consolidate my beginnings, my past pictures, as though they would over-expose, turn white in the darkroom of memory if I tarried too long in the present.

The days grew shorter as the book grew longer and the never-ending scroll of computer paper swirled around the room like a white seawave, gushing its way around dirty socks and empty cigarette packets. Records and CDs and old photos lay scattered between books open at random pages, along with the Thesaurus which my mum and dad had presented me with on my twelfth birthday. I threw open the windows and cranked up the heating full blast. I sat huddled in my cardigan and bedsocks and didn't bathe for days. I arched my back and lay silently on the floor, astonished to find I had been hunched over the machine for several hours without a break. Bewildered at the sharp ache in my lower back, I marvelled at my body's exhaustion. This body which could withstand roadside snacks on Bombay streets, nights of no sleep, lovemaking at dawn, endless cigarettes, strong black coffees with four sugars, drugs, food, flu and pre- menstrual tension, felt for the first time fragile. I must take care of myself, I thought dimly, and filled the bathroom cabinet with beroccas and aspirins and deep heat. I couldn't afford to fall ill, there was no time.

And one day, on a cold dark December evening, I finished my first novel.

The first person I told was Frank and he took it away with him to read during his lunch breaks and at night when he sent lovers away after making love with them. I slept for most of the week, too afraid to go outside or phone him, worried that I had isolated myself in the pursuit of indulgence. Gradually, I started cleaning up the flat, pushing the hoover around the corners which I now felt belonged to me. I dusted and wiped the bookshelves and arranged all my books in colours and height and authors. I gazed hungrily at all the little nick-nacks that Tash had arranged on the shelves – a white candle, a blue jug, a Moroccan lamp, little icons which had observed my achievements. I felt a sudden urge to talk to Luke, tell him that I wasn't just a poseur, I had become motivated and stopped watching the world go by with a sneer. The phone rang and I sprang to answer it.

'Hi!' Tash's voice was sunny and back to how it had always been.

My heart surged with happiness. 'Why haven't you called me, how's everything? I really miss you,' I shouted.

'Everything's good,' she said. 'Mum's gone into remission.'

'What? Wow!'

'It's just gone away. Did you know cancer can do that?'

We both burst out laughing.

'Really?' I said.

'Listen,' she said, 'I'm going away. I need a break. I need to get back to...myself.'

'Where to this time?' I asked in amazement. Whenever I had felt low or bogged down at university, I had phoned home to complain. RaviKavi asked what the matter was, was the work too difficult, were the tutors bad, hadn't I made any friends. I didn't know, I just felt low. Come home darling, Mum would say, just come home. Home had always been the place where I had got back to myself, even when it was the place that I was for ever plotting on leaving.

'Guess,' she said and sniggered.

'Not Injaaa!' I said. 'Bloody hell, all my friends are going to end up there while I'm left all alone in cold Blighty.'

Frank didn't phone, he came round. He told me without
any preamble, that he had given the manuscript to a guy
he'd met in a bar, who turned out to be a literary agent. It
was all perfectly kosher, he had checked him out.

'What do I need an agent for?' I asked.

Frank made an exasperated gesture. 'You don't know
anything. We go on holiday, I get us a discount with the
travel agent. You write a book, I prostitute myself so you get
it published. See how good I am to you?'

'What sort of name is Torquil?' I said suspiciously.

'What d'you want him to be called? 007?' said Frank.

Torquil the agent said that Asian writing was in vogue these
days and he was sure that he could sell it. I was shocked,
gobsmacked, devastated, delirious. I couldn't believe it could
be that easy, but Frank assured me that I worried too much.
He said we were all going to be rich and famous. He took me
out and got me drunk in various drinking bars in Soho and I
felt as though I was rediscovering my city. London was
dressed up for Christmas, over-dressed as usual. I gazed at
the wet silvery streets, mouths with steam coming out, the
smell of chestnuts, hurdy gurdy carols, twinkling shops and
cafés and scurrying umbrellas blown inside out. Everything
seemed fresh and new and good and when I spoke I could
hear myself breathless with excitement, drinking in the
night, feeling the city wrapped around me like a velvet cape
of good hope. We talked about the manuscript as though it
were already a book on a shelf and how we would arrange
it, display it, ask for it, order it, become overbearing parents
of the new arrival. I felt as though nothing could stop me,
that I was entirely invincible, made of some material that
could not stain or tear. Yet only three days before Christmas
Eve, I nearly lost my life.

I was strolling down the Tottenham Court Road, staring
at the glittering shop windows of Habitat and Heals, carving
my way through the hordes of shoppers when something
caught my eye on the road. It was Amrit, his profile

unmistakable, sitting in the back of a taxi! Going the other
way! My heart rocketed and without thinking I dived into
the road, and right into a chrome bumper. The ground
skidded under my feet, a screeching of brakes, a battery of
car horns. I jumped back, my legs jelly, my body drenched
with adrenaline. The driver was screaming abuse, and all I
could see were harsh lights.

And then out of the blue, there was Amrit holding my
arm. I felt as weak as dust. We stared at each other in the
middle of traffic, obscenities lashing around us.

'Are you intent upon killing yourself?' he said sternly.

'Sorry.' I was immediately chastened. 'Sorry,' I said,
leaning into the driver.

'Come on,' said Amrit leading me towards his taxi. He
took my elbow, in the same gesture he had used all those
months ago in Shaftesbury Avenue. It was useless to protest.
We moved seamlessly away from the carnage of confusion
and car horns. He manoeuvred me inside the taxi where I sat
with my knees shaking. His body was pushed up against
mine and he placed a protective hand on my back. He was
smiling.

'Alright?' he said softly.

'Yes,' I said, taking a deep breath.

'Where to?'

'Oh, I'll get the tube, I was just going home. It was my
fault.'

'It's alright,' he said reassuringly, and leant forward again
to speak to the driver. He took his hand away from my back
and firmly closed the glass partition. I was dazzled that he
should remember my locality and I smiled at him gratefully.
I had a sudden thought that my encounters with Amrit kept
happening in the square mile of Soho, and that each street
and landmark where we had met had already become
invested with some kind of emotional drama. The cool dark
restaurant in Meard Mews, the corner of Shaftesbury Avenue,
the dismal Despair in Romilly Street and now the bustling
furious Tottenham Court Road, where we were speeding

through cross town traffic towards my flat. I couldn't stop smiling and I looked out of the window so that he wouldn't see, wouldn't hear the butterfly fluttering of my heart.

'Are you going somewhere?' I said, turning to look at him. He had been watching me. There was a small overnighter at his feet.

'I've just got back. I've been away on a lecture tour,' he murmured looking into my eyes and I felt an inexplicable surge of wild excitement rip through my body. He had travelled through the mysterious skies and reached the ground and I had thrown myself in his way like an arrow of destiny.

'I'm fine, you know. I don't need... You don't need to go out of your way,' I stuttered, half afraid that he would take me at my word.

'Who is there, who is not in need?' he said and giggled.

When the taxi stopped outside my flat, he coolly asked if I had any alcohol upstairs. He asked the taxi to wait and walked obediently behind me with his overnighter as we climbed the stairs. I wanted to ask him if he wouldn't be late, where he lived, what he was doing here, but I didn't say anything. I wanted him to step over the threshold, be in my company, in my place. He poured us two long gins. I was all for drinking the gin straight, because I didn't have any tonic, but he said we had to at least have ice to water it down.

'Don't you ever defrost this bloody fridge?' he said.

We were staring at each other. He kissed me in front of the open freezer door. I kissed him back. The cold gust made us both shudder and giggle. He was smiling when I tore my face away from his. I started laughing and shut the freezer door, walked into the front room, onto firmer ground. He followed me.

'I don't believe this just happened,' I said.

'Let's make love,' he whispered, and this sent me into hysterical paroxysms of laughter.

'Listen.' I stroked his hair; incredulously it felt like wire wool, like horse hair. 'Listen you don't understand. I couldn't possibly do that. I mean you've got...' I touched his stomach. It bulged above his trousers. 'I mean look at this stomach. No, you don't understand. It's not within my comprehension.'

He was staring at me intently, his grey eyes unblinking. I looked at him and wondered what sort of seducer this man was. He looked very ordinary to me. Very quiet. Not shy, kind of sad, or rather removed. He seemed detached from things. I couldn't explain it to myself. I reached out and touched the side of his face. We looked at each other. Then he slid to the floor, got on his knees and took both my hands in his.

CHAPTER SEVEN

'I never thought you would ever let me kiss you,' he said.

'Why?' I asked.

'Because I didn't think it was ever possible. From the first time I saw you, that day when you came to the restaurant, in your bare legs and sandals. I thought, my god, who is she? I never thought...' He was grinning. 'You looked like a film star.'

I felt amused by his seriousness. We were drunk. It didn't feel like it was really happening, nothing to do with the ease I had with Luke.

'Do you have a hi-fi somewhere here?' he said.

I laughed. Hi-fi, what a word!

'There.' I pointed to the tape machine in the corner with its length of flex twined up with the television cord and tapes scattered around.

'I made a tape for you,' he said and walked over to the machine.

'When did you have time to make a tape?' I said, although I was happy and astonished that people still made tapes once they weren't students driving across town in battered old cars just to see sunsets in harbours.

'You're right,' he said sheepishly. 'I bought it in New York. I wanted you to think I had made it for you.' He sat down on the other side of the room, grinning at my perplexed expression.

A woman's voice, like tyres on gravel, fell into the room. The saxophone moving behind it, like a yearning shadow. I had heard it before, a vague background in some room on campus, a drone. Now, suddenly, the words were like still life compositions.

> Putting rain in my eyes
> Tears in my dreams
> And rocks in my heart.

We listened to the music without looking at each other. He was crouched by the tape machine. The sky crackled outside. I could feel the moisture in the air easing in through the open window, the faint chill of the breeze like a stranger's breath on my neck. What's happening to me, I thought.

> Till I'd be so bewildered,
> I wouldn't know what to do
> Might as well
> give up the fight again.

Again. I was thinking. Again. Again. But it wasn't like that for me. For me it was the first time. How could that happen, it was only a song? You didn't change because of a song. You didn't convert because of a word. There was a pressure in my head. I put my fingers to my temples and pressed hard against my skull. Amrit turned and smiled at me from the other side of the room. He turned down the volume.

'The first time I heard this, I thought I was the only person in the world, that I had been given special privileges.'

He came over to sit next to me. He touched my chiffon trousers, now sodden with alcohol and cigarette ash. Then he took his hand away and crossed his legs and put a serious expression on his face. 'So, tell me what kinds of things are you planning to do with your life, Miss Chowdhary?'

I burst out laughing, but I felt hurt. 'Have you given up trying to seduce me already?' I asked wide eyed.

He roared with laughter and gave me a bear hug. 'Oh, baby doll, you are the sweetest thing, man. Just to kiss you is so sweet.'

'Gross!' I screamed 'Whered' you learn that dialogue? Don't say things like that, it's embarrassing you know.'

'You're right,' he said slyly. 'It's sexist, isn't it?'

'You're trying to categorize me, suss me out, aren't you?' I said, remembering his retort at Matty's party. 'Well, I'll tell you something. It's not sexist, it's naff.' To emphasize my point I put two fingers inside my mouth and pretended to throw up. 'I thought you were a womanizer. Does that sort of thing work with women? What do they do, lie back and think of India?'

As soon as I had said the words I wanted to take them back. They weren't witty and ʻamusing as I'd intended. Cautiously, I glanced at him, fearing that any minute he would storm out. But he didn't do anything like that. He tilted his head and looked at me as if I were a painting and he was getting a perspective on it.

'What are you doing?' I asked quietly.

'I'm sailing without a plan,' he said.

'I'm sailing without a plan, what the hell does that mean?'

'I want more than anything to get inside the middle of you. Yes, yes, I know you're about to put two fingers down your throat because you think that's naff as you would say, but I know you're not going to let me, so that will be alright,' he said.

'Let you?' I said frowning. 'I've never thought of sex as something I let a man do to me. I thought it was something you did together. You make me sound like a fortification. Storming the citadel.'

He smiled at me, a really big smile, and put his arm around me as though I were a cousin.

'I like you, captain, I really like you, you know.'

I was frowning, processing furiously. 'This is your line,

isn't it? You seduce women by being enigmatic. That's what you do. Is that what you do?'

'Stop being so angry all the time,' he said.

'What's the matter? When did you stop getting angry, Amrit?' I said in irritation. I knew how melodramatic it must sound. How precocious it must seem to him.

'Oh somewhere back in 1972.' He said it so seriously that I felt off balance. I couldn't work out this man at all.

'Listen,' he said, 'I'm forty-seven years old. I've had a lot of relationships I suppose. You're absolutely right not to get involved with a decrepit old man like me, you don't know where I've been. I have two households, three children. I used to be married a hundred years ago to someone else. I am far too old for you, with nothing to offer, except perhaps an experience.'

I stared at him incredulously. I wanted to laugh and laugh and at the end of it, none of what he had said would be true any more.

'What if the experience leads me into pain, what shall I do?' I heard myself say.

'You have to trust yourself.'

'I don't know what you mean. I feel a bit mad. I'm not sure what's happening but I don't want you to leave until I know everything. There's a lot to know, isn't there?'

'Well, yes, there are books to read and learn from, there are countries to visit, compromises to be made. All that stuff you mean?'

'You know I don't mean that. I mean...I mean that suddenly I think I've got things to learn and know and I'm not even sure what they are.'

'No one does, that's the secret. That's why we read books and see plays and listen.'

'What do you mean you've got two households? What does that mean?' I said.

He leant back into the sofa and sighed. I remember how the room clicked into my head. My front room was suddenly different. The low light, the bare floorboards, the pale blue curtains which I'd had made up in India and carried back. They had weighed a ton and led to a big argument with my dad who warned me that if they charged excess baggage to bring all that material through Customs because it exceeded twenty-five kilos, I would have to abandon it with my uncle who had come to see us off. Implicit in this warning was the bald criticism that (as usual) I had not considered things, that (as usual) I had not thought of the consequences when I had exuberantly rushed into the tailor with reams of hand-woven blue cotton. 'It's so cheap, Dad.' 'You're in India,' he said, 'not in Habitat. You should compare like with like. No one here would think it was cheap.' 'But I don't live in India, Dad, I don't know what to compare it with, other than with Habitat.' RaviKavi had a policy about being Indian. Just because you live abroad, just because you are earning 'ponds', doesn't mean you can go to India and throw your money around. At the very least it shows a lack of culture. It gives you a respect which is not earned.

Amrit was sipping his gin thoughtfully. He shrugged. 'What do you want to know?' He sighed as if I were MI5.

I wasn't used to people answering a question with a question. I didn't realize that was his way of playing for time, assessing how much to reveal, measuring the impact. It didn't cross my mind that he must have had this conversation repeatedly with women in dimly-lit drawing rooms. I didn't know how tiresome it was for him, this preamble, because I thought that when lovers embarked upon each other's bones, everything was new and each said exactly what was in their mind. I had no idea there were other ways of being.

'I've just told you,' I said, irritated with his sigh, wanting to pull it back and make it different. 'Are you a Muslim? Is that why you have two households?'

'Of course I'm not. Of course I'm a Hindu,' he said. 'Like you,' he added.

'Like me?' I looked at him disbelievingly. 'You are nothing like me.'

'You would be surprised,' he said and smiled.

Perhaps at the dinner parties and seminars he went to, that passed for conversation, and his friends and associates knew about signals for changes of subject, but I knew no such things. I was an only child. I was not used to having information withheld. It was part of my upbringing.

'Were you married to a white woman?' I asked pointedly. It was just the sort of question that would infuriate me when it was spoken by my parents' friends. They always wanted to know if the girl was dark but pretty? Muslim? Hai Raam! Foreigner? What will become of the children? I used to think the educated secular people of my parents' circle wouldn't be interested in such low grade behaviour, placing people according to their race and class and creed. I liked to beat the drum of the brave new world, of inter-racial harmony and unite and fight, a smug-faced cat amongst their pigeon-toed conversations. 'English people,' I used to boast proudly, as though I had invented English people, 'don't care about those things.' 'Oh really,' my parents would say witheringly, 'English people are very cunning, they don't say things to your face.'

'Of course not. I was married to a respectable Indian girl,' he said, as though I should know this, what a silly question to ask. For some reason I felt enraged.

'Come on,' I challenged him.

'Yes,' he said slowly, 'I should tell you. I want to tell you. There are two women who I have babies with. I'm not married to either. That's all.'

I started to laugh. Duh-duh-duh-Dat's all folks! 'Like... baby mothers,' I said, 'like West Indian men do.'

He cringed. And I thought, despite his Englishness, his grooming, how Indian he is, how typical of so many other Indians I had met who balked at being included in 'Black People'. 'I'm not black', they would retort, shocked that anyone should think so.

'How come you didn't marry them? Or one of them?'

'It only happens once,' he said. 'One only marries once.'

'How did it happen? Tell me from the beginning.'

'Start at the beginning,' he said and sighed.

In the beginning, there was a city called Ayodhya in which lived a king called Rajah Dushrat, I was thinking. He had three wives. Their names were Kaushalya, Sumitra and Kaykee. Kaushalya, the eldest wife gave birth to Raam, who was to marry Sita, be banished unjustly to the jungle for fourteen years, and finally defeat Ravan in the mother of all battles, the battle between Good and Evil.

Ravi had once joked to one of the Visiting Gods that the story of the East was the story of Raam, the Ramayana, where Good triumphs over Evil, and the story of the West was the story of Hamlet: To be or not to be. Doubt. And the story of Amreeka, they had sniggered, was Dobedobedobe-do.

My father had taught me the story of the epic Ramayana when I was six years old. In Bombay where I was born, I would sit cross-legged on Kapoor auntie and uncle's bed and recite the whole thing to the gathered neighbours sitting and standing in doorways. From the beginning. It would amuse everybody. They all knew the story as well as they knew their family history. I was famous for it in our colony. The MRI colony. Mid-Range Income. Three sets of flats overlooking a square of green where boys played cricket and sometimes cows wandered in off the road. I would hang off the balcony and throw mango stones for them to finish off. I had been living in England for years, and the green had been built up into flats, and the veracity of Raam's birthplace was in dispute. Everything had changed.

'I was going with this woman,' said Amrit, 'I had a scene with her.'

'Why do people from the sixties always say that? Why do they talk about relationships so euphemistically?' I said.

'Am I to answer all your questions simultaneously?' he asked.

I laughed and stopped talking.

'I was seeing her, you know.'

'She was your girlfriend.'

He considered what I said, as though it was something to consider. I was watching him. His hair falling over his magnificent eyebrow, his movements so slow and assured. The glasses perched on the bridge of his nose giving him the look of an intellectual. I bet you were useless at sports, I thought suddenly. I bet you were picked on and people called you Four-eyes and you were a swot.

'Whatever,' he said. 'And then she wanted to have a baby.'

'Just like that?'

'Women do you know,' he said kindly. I was insulted as though he thought he had to tell me what women were like. Women as opposed to girls. 'We talked about it interminably. We'd screw and then talk about it. In the supermarket, she would provoke it, all the time. I didn't want all that. I was running around, man, I didn't want the bother of it. I thought it was wet. But she wanted to have a baby. And it was, to be precise, the seventies for your information.' He arched his eyebrow at me. 'Anyway, she said that she would have a baby and live with her sister and her boyfriend and some other people in another house. She had an income you know from her people. They would look after the baby communally. That's how people talked you know, then,' he said looking at my face.

All at once it seemed absurd to me to hear this, well, old man, talking about being young and casual. Yet at the same time, it seemed like a freer wilder world that he was painting. Dangerous, striding freedoms. I couldn't imagine stretching RaviKavi's allowance beyond food, drugs and mortgage repayments. I tried to conjure up the scene.

'What were you doing then? Were you already a writer?'

'Of course not. I was dragging out a Ph.D., rather half heartedly. I was trying to write a novel. Doing odd jobs, moving around on the fringes of radical groups. I'd always wanted to write, never dared to imagine I could. My father thought that writers were all homosexuals and thieves. Sharaabi kebabis!' He grinned. 'Anyway, I was seeing Jonesy at the time.'

'What sort of name is that?'

'Jones. Susan Jones. She was a social worker type person, helping disadvantaged immigrants. I'd met her around and about, you know. At meetings, things like that.'

'Was she the kind of white woman who hung out with black men?' I said, my eyes shining malevolently. 'One of those drab women, eager to be decent, to be free of prejudice?'

I didn't know why I'd said it. I'd heard that sort of remark on campus thrown at women with Palestinian scarves wound round their necks hanging on the arms of the men who formed the Black Student Alliance. I was never part of those crowds, never thought Race was anything to do with me. At a BSA disco I'd tried a scam. 'We're both Indians,' I'd suggested to the Indian student at the door, imitating RaviKavi who thought every Indian on the street was a potential acquaintance. 'Let us in free, go on.' 'What's Indian about you,' the man had sneered. 'Have you looked in a mirror recently? Indian women don't have blue hair and white boyfriends.' I had been appalled at that negation, protective of Luke who was standing shamefaced next to me.

Amrit looked at me for a minute and then lowered his head and scratched the top of his ear. 'Aren't you sharp? Like the crease on a trouser,' he said musingly, and I took it to be a compliment, an abdication to my superior assessments. Then he smiled wryly. 'I suppose she was.'

'And then? Then what happened?' I said with relish, the way you turn a page on a thriller, having stopped yourself for a few minutes to work out the denouement, eager to make your own imprint upon the plot.

'Clarissa knew about it. She still wanted a baby. It was cool. She knew I was seeing Jonesy because I wasn't interested in all that shit. Family and settling down. I said to her, fine you have a baby and I will do as much as I can. I will help you financially and practically but I come and go as I please.'

I thought about those names. I thought about the

familiarity he had with them. Jonesy. It was a pet name. Clarissa, it was a glamorous name. English girls. There was a film with Jack Nicholson called *Carnal Knowledge* that I'd seen on TV as part of a Movie Classics season. He was a playboy who had settled down with Ann Margret, but he still wanted to play the field. She was a model who had given up her career and grown fat and sad. She says to him, 'How come you're never here? How come I never know where you are?' He says, 'When I'm here, I'm here.' She says, 'And when you're not here?' Jack Nicholson throws something across the bedroom and turns his blazing eyes to her. 'Then I'm... Then I'm there.'

'Then?'

'Do you have any more alcohol?' asked Amrit. He got up and started to root around the table in the corner which served as my bar. Picking out a bottle of whiskey, seeing there was enough for a large one, he lumbered back towards me. I couldn't keep my eyes off him. The way he walked, so controlled. That smile, so far away. Out of reach. He poured the whiskey into my glass. I wrinkled my nose because it was Luke's bottle and I always found whiskey too sour, too adult. I sipped and thought, remember this. You'll think of this time when it's over between you. You'll tarnish it with all sorts of intimacies that aren't here. You'll look back to it with yearning. Memorize it. Know it. There was a stab inside my heart, as though I was standing in front of a tunnel and could see the end, but the light was not bright, it was murky. The only part of the tunnel that seemed to make sense was the dark.

As he sipped and put a casual arm around me, I knew instinctively that he had done this before. The same routine. I gulped the whiskey and pushed the idea from my mind. I tried hard to think of the other beginnings. Seeing him behind a sweep of shadows in the coolness of that restaurant. Standing with a glass of cold champagne, feeling foolish in my pillbox hat. The Despair and our words and our understandings and the Tottenham Court Road and near death and destiny. All those beginnings were finished. I realized with a jolt I was already in the dark.

'Are you alright?' He looked at me, full of concern. Just the way anyone would, after gin and whiskey. It was impossible to explain. My head was bursting.

'I'm a bit drunk if that's what you mean,' I said defiantly. 'But I'm still not going to sleep with you.'

He smiled and kissed the side of my face. 'Not until you have investigated me further, am I right?'

I couldn't tell if he was making fun of me or if he had read my inner thoughts.

'So where were we?' he said expansively and moved closer on the sofa. Heavy against my skin, he seemed to fill the room.

'Clarissa got pregnant,' I said impassively.

He sighed. 'She was living elsewhere. And then three months before the baby was due, the communal house fell through. Her sister broke up with her boyfriend, the others disappeared. The whole idea fell apart. Her people cut her off financially. So she turned up at my doorstep. One doesn't refuse someone who is in the later stages of a pregnancy. So she moved in.'

I was staring at the grainy floorboards. I didn't want to hear any more. The words had become lacerations. I didn't understand what was happening, but I couldn't stop listening. The story of his life was unfolding before me and I was afraid.

'What about the other one?'

'Jonesy? I was seeing her. Screwing her,' he said carefully. 'Jonesy couldn't have kids you see.'

I couldn't think of any sharp-as-a-crease-on-a-trouser retort to say. These women. I tried to imagine their faces. The colour of their hair. And this man was telling me about them and they didn't even know who I was. Their stories were part of his seduction of me.

'Then,' he looked at me and grinned as though he were telling me a cricket score, 'Jonesy got pregnant, just after Clarissa had a child.'

'I thought she couldn't...'

'Well, these things happen. To this day I don't know whether she was taking fertility pills or something. Maybe she was. She had twins.'

'Twins!' I exclaimed, in the way everyone does at that strange fascination of two peas in pod. 'How brilliant!'

He laughed and I wondered if I had been so effusive because that was how he preferred it. Light and breezy.

'Is that enough? Do you need to know more?' he asked, a concerned expression on his face.

CHAPTER EIGHT

'Don't analyse it all, why d'you have to analyse it all the time? Just shag him. I can't believe you even own a rucksack.'

I was steadying the chair as Tash reached into the recesses of my top cupboard. Luke had taken me camping for a weekend and it had been the site of our first row. Although I had set off enthusiastically in my new boots and backpack, imagining myself to be a traveller, the uncomfortable tent with the flapping door and the lack of running hot water had sent me reeling into the nearest B&B. I had stuffily informed Luke that they didn't teach survival skills in comprehensive schools. Knowing that I would have spent more money on the wardrobe than the fare, Tash had reminded me that I must have a rucksack that had fallen into disuse. As far as I was concerned, she was welcome to the grotesque item.

'This is great, it's brand new, is it really OK if I borrow it?' she exclaimed, jumping off the chair.

'Take it away, out of my sight,' I said as she flattened it out on the bed. She looked alive, her eyes glistening with anticipation. The crisis was over and the Burly Spaniard had transformed into a doting lover. She had escaped while the going was good.

'At least you'll have something stylish as you're roughing it overland,' I added morosely. She was right, I should have just shagged him instead of talking for hours.

'I'm not going overland, I'm flying Air India. I can't wait. Hey!' Her eyes lit up. 'This guy, do you think he could give me some tips on India? I mean I've got the *Rough Guide* and I've talked to loads of other travellers, but you know...'

'What?' I shrieked. 'I can give you tips about India, what do you think I am? You don't even know him and suddenly he's a big authority on tourism.'

'Oh yeah, right. You've already given me your tips, though. Stay at the Taj, take taxis everywhere and stay out of the sun,' said Tash rolling her eyes.

It was true. I had given her my idea of as perfect a holiday in India as I could imagine, a holiday I had never had, and never would. Staying in any hotel – let alone a Five Star – in India, would have been tantamount to the most wounding act of betrayal as far as my parents and relatives were concerned. Every time I had gone to India I had dragged along behind my parents, jumping trains and travelling third class as they had always done, staying in cramped conditions with my relatives who didn't have Western toilets or air conditioning. You can't see anything if you travel first class, my parents would chorus. There were compensations of course: jokes and spiralling anecdotes that led into the night as card games ensued in low-light carriages, on makeshift tables of suitcases; bustling routine continuing in the households where we became temporary residents. I would accompany my uncle or father or the servant in the daily excursions to the butcher, the tailor, the dairy.

In India, every man who was related to me, and many who weren't, uncles and cousins and friends, would take charge of all my daily amusements, be they getting tickets on the black market for an evening show; driving me on the back of a scooter to purchase Halal meat from the butchers

– see how cleanly they cut it; see what old Dilli used to look like; accompanying me to tailor, jewellery shops, artefacts stores. They would haggle on my behalf: 'Openly looting and fleecing, this is what Dilli has become now? Are you trying to cut my nose, in front of my niece?' I would delight in the psychodrama played by the traders: 'Please, saab, don't insult me further by asking reduction. Take it, take it free. Don't pay me a paise. Not a pie.'

My father and my uncles liked giving me tours. They would point out where they used to live as students, where they used to eat, what unpronounceable and inappropriate names the government had inflicted upon the English street names in a hollow bid for nationalism. Hastings Road was now known as Gopalswami Mudialiyar Marg, Cornwallis Street as Ragharachanira Road. Travelling sideways, they stood next to me protectively on buses which were so crammed men were hanging off the windows; my father didn't see why I should get a taxi when it was ten times the price of a bus ticket. All ordinary people travelled this way, just because I lived in England now, did not entitle me to turn into a memsahib. Ravi was unaware of a whole generation of Indians who had grown up in India in his absence who had never set foot on public transport. Whenever I had complained about eating roadside snacks with the rest of them, or drinking fresh sugarcane juice from a stall that I was convinced was typhoid-ridden, my dad had dismissed my reservations with a snort of derision. This is the real India, he would tell me; this is what you will remember.

If I ever got sick, which I frequently did, not from contaminated food, but from sheer over-eating, then my medicines would be home-made. Yoghurt and rice would be spooned down my throat, questions would be asked about my frequent visits to 'Pakistan' as they referred to it jovially. Quaint green bottles of a tonic called Amrit Dhara (Life Line) would be pulled out of cupboards and administered to me lovingly. I couldn't remember a single home we ever stayed in which did not possess these little bottles as well as Eno's salts and an Ayurvedic medicine for colds, called Joshina.

The rub was, that when I defiantly went to India by myself the year before entering university, stubbornly travelling to locations on the hippie trail, I had found the experience deflating and bewildering. I tried to hang with red-faced English people, going around in rags and drinking only bottled water (which I knew to be filled from taps), getting the wrong train tickets, losing money, meeting other travellers, eating only bland watery dahls mixed with plain rice, without pickles or chillies. All the time, I was perversely yearning for hot sizzling 'snakes' from roadside stalls which tasted so good, even when you knew you would be laid up in bed for the next three days. Finally I had returned to the fold of some relative's house to lie inside cool rooms with overhead Cinni fans and fluorescent band lights, and watched *The Bold and Beautiful* on the TV with everyone talking over the dialogue. I made them hoot with laughter at my stories of 'Westerners Enduring India' just as I had told tales about 'The English People', when my parents had pounced on me in N3 with questions about what I'd been given to eat in my friends' houses. What? my dad would declare in outrage. No garlic, no chilli? Going to India had never been what you could class as a holiday, more a shifting of location.

I always had an idea there was another India, the India of ease and air-conditioned rooms and langour, that was out of my reach. So I had shortformed it in my mind, located it in a Five Star hotel, and urged someone else to do it on my behalf. Then I could enjoy it vicariously. My dad commented that I had watched far too many programmes like *The Jewel in the Crown* and *The Far Pavilions* on TV. 'We used to laugh at them,' he told me once. 'We used to laugh at the British soldiers at the edge of the small town I grew up in. They looked so red and puffy and they couldn't even speak English properly.' They used to laugh a lot, my parents, snigger at people who they thought were hybrids, out of place, inauthentic. And was I like that too, a hybrid out of place, with a cockney accent and a yen for decadence, contradicting the deep-seated austerity of a country which had changed beyond imagination? And those sahib men, those Indians who spoke English like English gentlemen and used a fork to eat dahl and rice, what were they? The thought brought me back to Amrit, and Tash.

'Well, what do you think he does? He's a published author, he doesn't backpack around the place. He probably makes one trip to some dhaaba to eat greasy lamb curry with his hands and then he's back in the bar of the Taj drinking bloody foreign whiskey,' I said angrily.

'Why are you so pissed off with him, what's he done to you?' asked Tash suddenly concerned.

'He's too bloody old and he has this complicated life and all I'm ever going to be is on the fringes of it. And yet he's intrigued the hell out of me.' I had tried to summon up Luke's face, tried to pull myself back into the old feelings, but they seemed to have faded, along with his absence.

'Oh,' she smiled, 'is that all? I thought it was something serious. What about jabs? I want to have them all, but I don't want to be sick. And malaria tablets, they cost so much and they have side effects.'

'Don't bother, I never bother. But I've got an iron constitution, nothing makes me ill,' I said banging my fist on my chest like Tarzan. 'I never get anything more than an upset tummy from over-eating. You'll get ill. Buy the malaria tablets there, much cheaper. All the drugs are cheaper in India,' I sniggered.

It occurred to me that I had given Luke no pearls of wisdom about enduring India. In any case, Luke was going to India for education, not enlightenment or entertainment. We had been too aware of our separation, our taking different roads. Had I been thinking of Amrit even then, on that rainy night when we had drunk Calvados and begun splitting up?

'No, don't say that. I'm not going to drink the water, I'm only eating vegetarian food, and anyway...' She stopped and grinned sideways at me, 'I'll be in the process of being spiritually uplifted.'

'Oh god,' I said good-humouredly. 'You wait and see how far that gets you once you've been robbed and your skin's got burnt and you can't find a Western toilet,' I added darkly.

I couldn't remember why we had become friends, but I know that it was on the first day of the big school and she had decided we were to be friends. Her shattered family was so different to my home full of parents chattering and cooking, playing host to the constant visitors from India who stayed and stayed. I had been led to believe that for the Hindu, the guest is god and I had seen more gods at close quarters in our semi-detached in N3, than I had ever seen in the Mid Range Income colony in Bandra. Where once we had lived amongst clerks and managers and schoolteachers speculating about Foreign, in London we welcomed gods who constantly talked of India. There was nothing stronger than the umbilical cord of the past, nothing more potent than the rope of familiarity, nothing as sure as home. This relentless marination led to the coating of your character with strength and vigour and gravity. Without the endless layers – of family, tradition, acts of good faith – you became a drifter, a person in search of himself in an alien land. This was the unwritten constitution of my parents, yet I was constantly on the lookout for getting swamped by an alien culture.

'But maybe it's dangerous territory. Perhaps I shouldn't go there. I mean this guy's not a good bet, is he?' I said after telling her the whole story.

'Then don't go. You don't have to go at all, I agree it could well be risky. You're the one saying it's dangerous, I don't know what lurks there, I'm not going; but you desperately want to go. So go. Be fearless. Get some jabs,' she laughed triumphantly. 'Be a traveller for once in your life.'

I was smiling, the idea was attractive. The thing was, what would I save if I didn't enter this terrain and what would I lose?

'The stomach, I have to say, would be a problem for me,' she laughed.

We were sitting in exactly the same positions on the sofa as I had sat with Amrit the night before, and today everything looked clear. The room was back to normal.

'So you talked and talked and then he left?' she said disapprovingly.

'We kissed,' I conceded.

'So nothing really happened. Why are we discussing it?' she said.

'The taxi. I mean he kept it waiting for two hours,' I said eagerly. Just the sheer wastage of money was a big thrill to me.

We had kissed at the door and he had asked if we would continue like this. Would I go and have lunch with him and pretend it's all the same? I'd said I didn't know. He said he was a lecturer in a university in Russell Square. He had given me his numbers. There were so many of them.

'What does it mean, sailing without a plan?' I asked. 'Do people have plans when they have relationships?'

'When they have affairs I suppose they do.'

'Affairs?' I let the word swim around my mouth for a bit. It felt delicious and obscene. 'But silly women have affairs, don't they?'

She was irritated now. 'Why don't you just have a look? If you don't like it, get out. It's not as if you've never had a relationship before.'

Yet I was already in a different place, looking out over a momentous scene. Mist everywhere. Everything was different. There was no map.

It was three days to Christmas and everyone was rushing around in the tinkling streets buying trees and presents. It gave me a strange feeling to think of Amrit moving about in West London. I had asked him which house was home. He said, both. He said I could call him wherever I liked and he'd call me when he could. How did he spend Christmas, did he have two dinners, turkey twice? No, he told me, it worked out differently every year: pheasant at one place, goose at the other. I couldn't stop thinking about it, the way he spoke, the way he recited his life, with such insolence. What sort of an Indian was he? That accent. A sahib man. Received pronunciation. Picking out a Chardonnay. Two women. What did his mum and dad think about it all? Well, he was nearly fifty years old, but he was an Indian, so he must have parents who had opinions about his life.

I couldn't wait for Tash to leave so I could make a call. I was embarrassed about it. I wanted no witnesses.

'Hello,' he answered, 'are you having a nice Christmas?'

I didn't know what to say. The Christmas holidays he meant, I supposed. My heart was beating. I had expected him to say don't call me here.

'Can I see you soon?' I blurted out.

'Why don't you come up to the university on Boxing Day? For a drink.'

There was something so assured in his tone. I imagined him in a room full of decorations and children and the mother of his children and him talking casually on the phone to a girl he had kissed in a room. Something about the scene devastated me, like a tragedy on TV in your warm sitting room.

The post arrived in bursts, throwing collections of cards on the mat. Amongst them was a large A3 envelope, which I ripped open excitedly. It was *Pinned* magazine. I turned the pages slowly, deliberately, until I saw the photograph. I stared at it. Luke's arm around my shoulders, my hands around the coffee cup, outside Bar Italia. The light was so bright, the image so bleached out that it looked like a scene suspended in time. It was a strange magazine, its entire contents seemed to be photographs. We were one of many. I didn't know what to do with it, felt it was wrong somehow to throw it away. Yet I knew I would never look at it.

Somehow Christmas passed. There was no one to talk it over with, because everyone was with their family, even Frank.

Matty and Ralph were in Egypt, they had sent me a card. Re-runs of movies on TV. I didn't want to talk. I wanted to be alone. RaviKavi had never made any concessions to England and so, unlike other Indians and Jews that I knew, we had never celebrated Christmas, not even for show. Even when I was young and wanted to be like the rest of the kids in the class, my parents thought the idea of buying a Christmas tree and cooking turkey faintly ridiculous. Their only concession was to give me a present. But some years they forgot and after a while there was nothing I really needed. Over the years, I was glad of their non-conformism, because it meant I could do what I liked over the holiday.

I took a walk on Christmas Day in the woods behind my flats. It was mossy and damp. Behind the thick lattice of branches I could see windows twinkling with trees. And I could almost hear the crackers and the jokes told around the dinner table before people settled down to the Queen. I remembered the Christmasses of my childhood when, fresh to England, I had peered into those lit up houses. Mummy, can't we have a tree? Why do we have to have meat curry? I want turkey. My mum was clever. She had no inclination to recreate an authentic Christmas for me but, as they say, she knew a man who did, friends she had made in the Legal Aid Centre where she 'solicited', as my father liked to joke. Ravi of course had no English friends at all because he worked in the India Office passport section, where all his colleagues brought parathas and puris for lunch and shared them out.

My mother's friends invited us to their houses, and I spent several Christmasses in the company of upper middle-class English people. They weren't small sad affairs over Woolworth crackers, but lavish lingering afternoons playing charades, with mulled wine and sixpences in puddings, and long walks across still parks. One of her friends was married to a Jamaican man, and their Christmas had been a tidal wave of English Christmas trimmings as well as ackee and saltfish and roast pork and rice and peas and rum for everyone. I thrilled to those times when I had been a guest at the celebration of other cultures. So many things to learn and compare and no responsibilities.

That day, my head was full of how it would be when I saw him on Boxing Day. I walked for miles. The cold clung to my skin and the woods were desolate. There was a tight feeling in my stomach when I thought of him laughing by his Christmas tree, driving to another house, kissing mutual friends. Questions ricochetted against the walls of my head like exploding missiles. Did the women know each other, did they all have the same friends, how did it work? And what about the wife, the respectable Indian girl he hadn't talked of at all? Was there a rota? Was love distributed between the households, like the kheer divided between Rajah Dushrat's wives?

Stop now, stop it now, you don't know what you're getting into. Go on, go and see what he can give you to learn. Go and see. As I tramped the ground underneath me, my breath escaping in bursts, all at once he seemed to me another culture and my own culture at the same time.

CHAPTER NINE

I was one hour early for lunch. My hand was shaking, the waistband of my trousers sticking to my stomach. I sat in an empty coffee bar. The only people about in Russell Square in the light rain were dog owners and foreign students with umbrellas scurrying past the faded Imperial Hotel.

'Say, bella, you look be-uti-fool,' said the waiter pulling on the bubbling Gaggia machine. The place smelled reassuringly of burnt toast and roasting coffee beans, but his words made my heart sink.

'You look like you're in love,' he said.

Maybe they said those kinds of things to girls having coffee alone. Women, I told myself.

'He's a very lucky man.' The waiter was relentless. I gritted my teeth to make him stop. I wanted his chance remarks to stop burning into profound meanings. I made sure I was late. Ten minutes. Not too late. Just in case.

The university was a shabby grey building, full of corridors and noticeboards, similar to the university I had attended. I hadn't ventured into my tutor's offices more than a couple of times. All our dealings had happened in classes.

Following the principle of schooldays, my friends and I hadn't fraternized with tutors. At my university, all the tutors drank in the university bar and the students drank in the Union bar.

Amrit was at the photocopier when I turned into the corridor. On the ceiling were a series of squat fluorescent squares that lit up one after the other as I walked through. There was nobody else about, all the doors in the corridor were shut, bar one. The whirr of the photocopier seared the air.

He looked up, smiled, gestured towards the open door, and went back to his work. I walked past him into his office and sat down carefully on the sofa. On the edge of it. Everything was different. I avoided looking at any of the posters or the memos. Finally, he came in and sat down opposite me in his chair.

'Would you like a drink? I can open a university wine. It's not bad,' he said conversationally.

I hadn't eaten, I felt faint, but I said yes.

'Do you like teaching?' I asked, remembering the glazed expressions of tutors at my university.

'Sure. But I only take MA students now.'

'Why?' I said.

Amrit made a dismissive gesture. 'Undergraduates run home and tell their mummies if you say fuck.' He grinned.

I opened my mouth to protest, to stand up for all undergraduates everywhere but then I thought better of it. I would have raced proudly to RaviKavi with the news if I had heard such delicious transgressions.

'So, are you well?' he said, passing me a glass.

'I wanted to...er...go shopping. In town. That's why I thought I'd kill two birds with one stone.' It seemed important to have a reason for being there.

He was nodding. 'What do you want to buy? Everything's shut.'

'A coffee table. I saw one in the Reject Shop. Duck-egg blue. Reduced.'

'Well, why don't I help you?' he smiled. 'I can give you a lift. I could help you take it back to your flat... Unless?' He looked at me with his head tilted.

'Really?' I looked up into his eyes, my face breaking into a grin. It was going to be alright. He was an older person. He knew about protocol. He wouldn't let me get hurt. He would protect me from danger. All these realizations gave me an intense relief from the small talk we had been conducting. Automatically I reached inside my bag for my cigarettes. He had turned away for a few moments to shuffle some papers on his desk. I was so busy staring at his back that with a mounting horror I realized that instead of my packet of Bensons, I had pulled out the square blue box of Lil-lets! Before I had a chance to fling them back, he spun round and his eyebrows lifted like trapdoors. Remembering my previous embarrassment over the match trick, I held the square box in my hand and picked out a small cellophane-wrapped tampon, just like I would have picked out a cigarette. He seemed to be transfixed by my action and suddenly it occurred to me that he had never seen a woman extracting a tampon in quite this way, so brazenly.

'Just a minute,' I said and, closing my hand around the little thing, I strode out of the room, lest my courage abandon me. When I got inside the toilet, I threw the offending item in the bin and pressed my back against the door, my heart hammering. I replayed the incident in my mind frantically. Had I sent out messages without meaning to? Had I been cool and sophisticated, a little wild even, or had I been vulgar, common? I tried to think of a similar incident in my memory to compare it with but there had never been such a situation, nor such a feeling. Luke had been despatched to buy tampons. With Luke I had shared gruesome stories of menstruation, laughing and squirming over them together. But Amrit was not a boyfriend. He was never going to be a boyfriend that you kicked with your sockky feet in a cold bed to go make the tea.

We bought the table and I watched him load it into the

boot. I kept thinking he would say something or do something and I wanted to be ready for it. Instead, he talked breezily about bargains and the music on the radio and how well he knew North London. Back in my flat, I made coffee, and we sat on the sofa with our feet on the new coffee table.

'Someone was talking about your short story,' he said. 'At the university. They said it was rather good.'

I was shaken, I had forgotten all about the short story which I had won money for. It had been published in some obscure literary magazine. I couldn't wait to tell him I had written a novel now as well.

'What did you say?' I asked.

'I said, of course. Mira Chowdhary is a very talented writer. I know her.'

I laughed and he laughed.

'Do you think I'm a talented writer?' I asked archly.

'I don't know,' he said. 'You haven't written anything yet.'

I was perplexed. I didn't know it then, but there were to be several conversations between us where I understood nothing.

'You mean I don't have a body of work?'

'Something like that.'

'I've written my first novel,' I boasted.

He arched an eyebrow, it seemed to amuse him.

''Course it's not published or anything...But I just sat down and did it. It only took me three months.'

Amrit burst out laughing and my mouth fell. I didn't understand what he was laughing at.

'It took me five years to write my first book,' he said and smiled, and immediately I felt foolish. Proper writers who had something to say took time over their work. 'It took me almost another five to realize that I was no novelist,' he chuckled. 'I should have taken more notice of the reviews.'

'Did you read it? My short story?' I asked hopefully.

'I didn't have the time,' he said.

He was sitting in the same position on the sofa but it was daylight and the comfort of the dark was gone. There were so many things I needed to know and in the pit of my stomach it felt as though my life depended on it. At the same time, I felt a wave of tiredness that ate into my bones. I felt myself marooned at the edge of a landscape.

When he was leaving (to pick up one set of children from violin class) I provoked an argument at the door. He had kissed me and not even suggested that we sleep together. I was insulted and flattered. At any rate, I didn't want him to leave. Not just yet. Not before more questions could be answered. The first time Luke and I had talked all night, he had smiled at the door and said, 'When again?', but Amrit had already left, on to the next thing. He was taking his leave politely as I suppose he had been brought up to do.

'Your kids are middle-class English kids, aren't they?' I said accusingly. As soon as I spoke I wanted to take the words back because I knew I had no right to make judgements on his real life.

He smiled and shrugged as though it didn't matter at all what I thought.

'Can't they even speak Hindi? What sort of Indians are they?' I continued recklessly.

He was trying to leave. He was trying to be nice about it. 'Stop being so angry,' he said. 'I'll phone you.'

I walked with him down the stairs. I wanted to say something, a word, a sentence that would stay with him like an imprint. I pulled at his sleeve. He looked back at me, his face wan. He's tired of me already, I thought.

'I can't sleep with you,' I said urgently.

'That's alright.'

'Don't you want to have sex with me? Isn't that what this is about?' I said crossly.

'I can have sex wherever I like.'

'Oh,' I said, taken aback.

He was at the outside door now. He was nearly at his car. He smiled and I noticed how his teeth were ill-shapen and nicotine-stained. Like tombstones. His hair was falling seductively over his eyebrow. His skin was pale and soft.

There was no evidence on his face of cruel acts.

'Would you like me to say I have never had sex with anyone else?' he said, looking into my eyes.

'Doesn't matter,' I said turning away from him. He had humiliated me. I didn't know how it was possible. To hurt the people who liked you. To do it deliberately.

'Why don't you just have fun? Stop taking things so seriously,' he said as he got into his car.

'Alright then,' I said sulkily. But I wasn't sulking. Something was breaking inside me.

'I really do like you, you know. I really do like you,' he said.

I didn't know what to do with myself once he was gone. I looked at the coffee table and his cup. The room was quiet and hideous and I wanted to go somewhere else. Tash would be boarding the plane now. She had said the same thing to me, it felt like a conspiracy. Just have some fun, stop being angry. It was all a plan, I knew it. This was how he was doing it. Trying to get me into bed by saying he didn't want it. Gradually, by intriguing the hell out of me, he would make his path smooth for himself. The odd thing was I couldn't stop thinking about it. I thought about the way he kissed me and the things he said and what it would be like to feel him close to me. I thought about the way he spoke of sex and how dirty and old-fashioned it sounded: I'd like to get inside the middle of you. It made me squirm. Funny, odd to hear those words coming from the same mouth that asked if you would like a university wine. No one spoke like that, no one I knew. They were B-movie lines. The evening rolled by and I realized I had sat in the same place surrounded by thoughts and the creeping darkness of evening already settling in the room. I was clearing up the coffee cups when the phone rang.

'I'm at the airport,' she said.

'Oh Tash, I wish you weren't going. Take care of yourself. Forget everything I said. Take every precaution,' I shouted into the phone.

'I never listen to a word you say, you know that,' she said and we both laughed.

'When?'

'It's delayed. It's OK. Listen I just wanted to tell you. It's been running around my head since we saw each other.'

'What?'

'Don't listen to what I said. Don't think I didn't understand. To love someone so much you're consumed by them, there's nothing else in life.'

'What!' I shouted angrily.

'There's nothing else,' she said. 'Grab it, don't look back, don't worry about how long it will last. Don't think for a minute.'

'Shut up,' I said and giggled nervously. 'It's nothing like that.'

'OK,' she said. 'Good.'

We laughed.

'You can call me reverse, I don't care. But write me a postcard at least. You have to go to a post office to get it stamped, otherwise it'll never reach. It isn't the Royal Mail. You sure you've got Mum and Dad's address? Call them immediately you start freaking out.'

'Let me get on the plane first,' she laughed. 'I'll see you in six months.'

The mugs were clattering in my hands as I tried to carry them into the kitchen. The room became a blur, and tears welled up in my eyes. I sucked in my lips so that I didn't cry. Everyone was in India. All the important people. Do the washing up, watch a movie, then cry. The phone rang again. I ran for it. I was laughing as I put the receiver to my ear. She'd forgotten one last thing. As always, our goodbyes were protracted.

'Hello, it's Amrit Kaushik,' he said.

It hit me like a thunderbolt and I sank to the floor, but I was quick to regain my composure.

'Why do you say your full name, like it's a business call?' I said nastily. I didn't want him to think I was excited.

'I'm sorry, it's just a professional habit. I just didn't want to say it's Amrit. I didn't want to presume a familiarity.'

I laughed at his strange logic. How familiar did you have to be before you used your first name?

'Why did you phone?'

'Just to see how you are. And because I'm sorry about giving you short answers when you need long ones.'

'What does that mean?' I said in irritation.

I was beginning to think that although we both spoke English, we spoke in different dialects. It wasn't that way later, when we spoke in Hindi, as we sometimes did in the middle of phone conversations. I never realized that he was using those foreign words so that the women and children in the room wouldn't understand. I thought he was using them to bring us closer together, stand on the same piece of rock.

'Why don't you say things straight?'

'I don't know how to say those things. I'm a little afraid of you.'

'Are you being funny?' I said guardedly.

'Never mind. What are you doing?' he asked breezily. He laughed and it sounded to me like contempt, but I didn't care. Even if he wasn't going to express himself, that didn't mean I couldn't.

'I'm scared, Amrit, I don't know what I'm getting into.'

'It'll be alright. I won't do anything to hurt you,' he said and I believed him.

'What if I sleep with you and then fall in love with you and then I have nowhere to go because I will only be on the fringes of your life?' I blurted out.

'What if you fall in love with me anyway, even if we don't make love? Then what?' he said, and I could tell he was smiling at the other end of the phone and I didn't know the answer to that question.

'I do want to sleep with you,' I said and laughed.

'Good,' he said without a trace of emotion, and at the back of my mind I thought he's won, he's won me over.

CHAPTER TEN

The next day, the agent Torquil phoned to tell me he had got kicked out of the company. He was diabetic, and had unwisely drunk too much at lunchtime and thrown up all over their most prestigious author's lap. He had been told to leave immediately. So much for the Christmas spirit and the English reputation for fair play. I felt rather sorry for him as his awkward apologies spilled out of the phone.

'Don't worry,' he said. 'Don't lose hope. I still think it's a great book. There are other companies. I'll get back on track soon.'

'OK,' I said disinterestedly. It had all been too good to be true. I hadn't really believed that it was possible to get a book published that easily via a man Frank had picked up in a bar. In any case, I was too distracted to care.

I was glad I was going away for the New Year. I had learnt from our previous holidays that Frank went on holiday to sleep. All he wanted to do when he went abroad was to sit in cafés, lie on the beach (two hours max – not for a second did he want to be confused with other British tourists) and sleep. I liked to tag along, discarding my skin of guilt behind me.

RaviKavi had drummed into my head the importance of sightseeing, and as a little girl they had dragged me around museums and places of interest, mainly on our India trips. It was all part of their philosophy of Value for Money, which applied not only to living within your means, but also to getting the maximum 'enjoyment' and 'knowledge' from a budget. It was my dad's favourite Law of Economics, a subject he had been forced to study instead of his beloved Hindi Literature. Needless to say, after gaining his degree and satisfying the family, he had taken a job in the Civil Service and completed his Ph.D. in Hindi Literature, and written poetry in his spare time. There was a duty to your family and to society and then there was a duty to your self. He thought it was everybody's vocation to fulfil both. What he didn't understand was that there were people in the world who lived their whole life without ever having any concept of duty.

One such person was Frank. The thorny dilemma of foregoing sightseeing tours was solved by his choice of holiday location. We went to places where there was absolutely nothing to see. Frank had found a resort in Southern Spain. His aged spinster aunt went there every year to paint in the mountains, and we had rented an apartment on her advice. She had promised us there would be no lager louts or Euro discos. It was remote and quiet and full of sedate middle-aged German tourists, so there would be nobody we wanted to make friends with, an added bonus. Frank and I had decided to take some good books and celebrate the New Year leisurely over a bottle of Cava on the beach. Like grown-ups.

The day before the flight, Amrit came to my flat. He had a parcel with him. My bed was covered with all the clothes from my wardrobe and it looked like Beirut.

'Are you taking all those clothes?' he said curiously. 'They're all black.'

'I don't know what to take, so I put everything out on the bed and see what I like. I want to take everything, but there won't be anywhere to go and I'll just end up carrying it around aimlessly.' I was twittering away, happy that he was standing in my room and scrutinizing my clothes.

He nodded with a serious expression on his face as if I was saying something interesting. He was a published author, a university lecturer, he went abroad five times a year, he travelled all the time to places in England. He lived out of suitcases and hotel rooms. Even when he wasn't travelling, he was on the hoof, going from one house to the next, ferrying children and women to violin classes and dinner parties and weekends away. I felt ashamed at having such a small life.

'I thought you might like to read something,' he said, and handed me the parcel.

Excitedly I ripped it open and saw a hardback cover of his book.

'That's great,' I said and stuffed it into my bag. Then I whipped it out again and flipped the cover to see what inscription he had put there. There was none. I felt disappointed, suddenly so disappointed I couldn't speak. It just seemed like another book he had plucked from his collection and handed out. There was nothing personal about it. Maybe he had a hundred books at home on his bookshelf. The Visiting Gods would constantly be picking out anthologies from the sagging dilapidated bookshelf in RaviKavi's house. They would say, lolling their heads, 'This is mine now. You have insulted me enough by not gifting it earlier.' Consequently, neither my mum nor my dad had any copies of their own poetry books left in their possession. When asked to recite in company, they would demur and then irritatingly remind the other of an opening line. My father knew all my mum's poetry off by heart, all the poems she had written before they got married. In those days I used to think that books one had written were dispensable. What mattered was other people's wish to own them, quote from them.

'Is it one of your freebies?' I said, dropping it back in the bag.

'No,' he said with a hurt expression on his face, 'I went out and bought it especially.'

'Why didn't you sign it then?'

'I thought you would think that was...what do you say, naff?'

I liked the idea that he may have thought that really I was rather sophisticated. I leant across and touched his face and a shudder went through my body. His eyes were so pale and empty. I'll never stop getting a kick out of an Indian man with grey eyes, I thought. I remembered my sharp intake of breath the first time I had heard an Indian person speaking French. Oh la la, quelle tamasha! I opened my mouth to tell him that absurd anecdote and then firmly shut it again. It was childish to be surprised at every ordinary thing that happened all the time. He seemed so impenetrable. I had a feeling there was a huge amount to know and unravel. Perhaps there would be answers in his book.

'What's it about?' I said trying to sound casual, knowing that was a stupid thing to ask a writer. Either they would clam up completely (so many things) or else they would burst your brain with intricate plot scenarios. But that was in the past. All the writers I had met were my parents' friends, waving their hands like demented windmills and jay walking in the streets.

'People like us,' he giggled and turned around to walk out of the bedroom, as though it had been too easy to get my attention.

And I thought: I will have to use another method to make him love me. Let him patronize me, let him show me a different way of being. I made coffee and we sat with our feet tucked in by the coffee table.

'Nice,' he said and carefully placed his mug on a coaster.

No one ever used the coasters in my flat and I thought, I bet his house is well organized and he does the washing up before going to bed and I bet his kitchen doesn't smell of turmeric and chillis and garlic. When I was growing up, I remember always being embarrassed by that smell as it clung to my coat and my hair. I used to come home from school and race upstairs to put my coat in the bedroom so it wouldn't reek. When I had made no friends at the school and my father was sitting at the kitchen table with his head in his hands trying to figure out a way to make me happier, I would silently accuse that smell of garlic, hold it responsible, and both my parents responsible by association. I don't know when it was, but at some point after my parents had returned to their country, I started looking forward to that smell.

Now it smelled of home. I would cook dahl and lace it with a sizzling tarka, a concoction of seared garlic and chillies, and breathe in the aroma. I would mix it with steamed Basmati Rice, Tilda, (none of your Uncle Bens was found in our house) and sit cross-legged, naked in front of the TV and eat till my stomach groaned.

'Do you eat Indian food?' I asked him suddenly. 'At home, I mean.'

'Of course,' he said indignantly. 'Sometimes,' he added apologetically. 'When I cook it.'

'Don't your women know how to cook?'

'They're English,' he said.

'What do you eat? Brie and bread and tomatoes?' I asked eagerly. It thrilled me to think he could appreciate European food. My parents, and every other Indian I had met around that age group, reacted to eaters of non-Indian food with unbridled pity.

'They're not my women,' he said and turned his face away from me.

'Yes they are,' I said defiantly.

'Give me a ring when you get back,' he said.

He was so casual about it. He didn't even take hold of my hand. He's decided, I thought. He thinks I'm not worth the bother. I'm too inexperienced. I'm too young for him. He's going to pretend that nothing ever happened between us. Nothing had. Tash's words came back to me. What's the big deal?

And then suddenly I remembered Matty at the birthday party. Like a flying jigsaw, the expressions on her face collected in my mind, the lunch, the spoon rotating inside her coffee cup. I looked at Amrit, suddenly furious with jealousy.

'You had an affair with Matty, didn't you?'

His eyelids flickered. He shrugged. 'I had a scene with her a long while ago. That's all over now.' He smiled.

'Don't fucking say you had a scene with her. You had an affair with her. Did you or didn't you?'

'Yes,' he said simply, 'but why...'

'Yeah,' I said viciously, 'she was telling me. You were in a hotel in London. You kept going out to the car to get a light.' He smoked too much, she had said. He had bought her a scarf. I remembered her saying so.

'What's up with you?' he said.

'You bought her a scarf,' I said ridiculously.

'What does it matter to you? It's so unimportant,' he said in astonishment and I wanted to cry because he didn't know, because he was casually seducing me through his indifference and he had no idea about anything. I had felt sorry for her, and now I felt humiliated. Luke must have known about them, and in his own way he had tried to warn me. That's why he'd refused to learn chess. Amrit had consoled Matty, they had had an adventure and now they were civilized friends. It made me sick.

'It doesn't matter to me,' I said. I couldn't even get the sentence out, I was so jealous. I knew how unreasonable it sounded, but my head was burning.

'Oh,' he said. He looked at me and scooped me into an embrace. Suddenly he held me very tight and I began to cry. I couldn't stop. We didn't speak.

'I love you, I love you, I love you,' he said.

I felt as though he had pushed me into a dark hole and all I could do was fall. His words were lost in the world which was not mine any more. And yet, those words that came from his mouth, they seemed like exquisite pearls. I was too afraid to touch them, make them mine. It's not true, I thought. He says it to all the girls. They weren't pearls, they were mercury. Once I broke a thermometer and the little snails of mercury slithered out on the settee. 'Don't touch them,' said my mum, 'mercury is poisonous.' Inside the glass barrel, the silver liquid had looked so solid and functional, rising and falling with the temperature, contained and obedient.

'I know you don't think I mean it. One day you'll know I do.'

I sniffed back my tears, feeling cold and angry. His words were like an obstacle course waiting to baffle, stun, trip and trap. Words weren't words any more, they were means and ways of effecting emotions. They seemed to be proper English words, you could look them up in the dictionary and then suddenly they were dismembered letters, scattered on a Scrabble board, unknowable. Nothing was literal and all meaning had to be extracted. He's trying to dismiss me, I thought wildly. He's trying to dismiss me with his words.

'Is that the line you use on all the girls?' I asked him, lighting a cigarette. My tone was sour and my face was set in bitterness against him.

His expression changed. He smiled. His eyes were hooded and his skin was smooth. 'There are different lines for different girls,' he said.

Then before I could explode, he put his hand over my head. It felt so warm and hot and I wanted it to stay there always like a protective hat against further harm. He wasn't laughing any more. He was looking at me as though I was miles away. As though he was trying to understand something.

CHAPTER ELEVEN

'And it's too late, baby, now it's too late,' sang Frank as we drove towards the airport. The sun was shining and we had the roof down despite the cold breeze.

'Though we really did try to make it. Something inside has died and I can't hide and I just can't fake it,' we sang together and laughed.

In the plane he took two travel sickness pills, drank three brandies and conked out. He said it was the only way he got any peace and quiet from me. I felt safe and steady as the plane careered through the clouds with Frank's gentle snores purring next to me. The holiday would clear everything up. I comforted myself with the fact that somewhere, thousands of miles away, Luke was sitting in a seminar concentrating, Tash was marching along a Delhi street with the rucksack on her back, RaviKavi were dithering about the flat, puzzling over the architect's paperwork. Matty and Ralph were happy and together again. It was possible to avert disaster, I thought, clutching my seat belt.

The apartment in Spain overlooked the sea. We unpacked all our clothes immediately. Our toiletries, pooled together, crowded out the small bathroom. The first thing we did was get changed and go down to the beach café. It had lots of tables sunk in sand and little lanterns strung across the door. There were several people already drinking and eating under the afternoon sun. Men with stomachs protruding from their swimming trunks, women with sagging breasts. They had deep tans and spoke rapid German.

'When a man says. Does it mean?' I said, looking at the sea.

'Men lie. All the time,' said Frank.

'Yes. But when...'

'When you say you love someone, it can mean you love the feeling at the moment or it can mean I can't think of another word,' said Frank chewing furiously.

'I don't believe you,' I said and pursed my lips at the sun.

A little way from our table was a small middle-aged man, with a clipped moustache, smoking thin foreign cigarettes which smelt of cloves. His companion was a large muscular woman in a yellow swimsuit and white robe, her blonde hair piled up into a chignon. She was smoking a man's pipe and he was engrossed, nodding as she jabbered away in a strange language and poured wine out of their never-ending carafe. They looked like they had been rooted to the spot for days. It was not very warm but we ate a big plate of gambas with a jug of Sangria and sat in our shorts, speculating about the couple, as the sun set in front of our eyes. The pipe woman was still jabbering away as the sky turned mauve and red.

'You must be careful,' said Frank. 'He's not a reliable person.'

'I know,' I said glumly.

'If you were more like me, then I'd say you should go ahead, but you're falling in love. You can't fall in love with a man who will never be able to give you anything.'

'Why not?'

'Because you believe in all that romantic nonsense. I've known you too long. I know you think this is the man of your dreams and he isn't. He's just another married man who is dishonest and without honour. Luke's a good man. He loves you.'

'Let's go back, I'm freezing,' I said.

I made him move his bed next to mine, so I could see his face. We lay side by side with our books and talked to the ceiling. Frank made me laugh all the time. He had a different view of life. He spent hours on himself, putting on creams and facepacks without any embarrassment. He didn't believe in true love. He only believed in the ten-year man. He ate huge bowls of fruit salad and ran to the toilet every morning like a man possessed.

I opened Amrit's book. '*The Journey of One of Many*,' I murmured. There was no dedication I noticed with satisfaction. I turned to the back and looked at the photograph. 'Do you think he's good looking?' I said, showing Frank the flap.

'What's that got to do with it?' said Frank.

I flipped through the book. I wanted to find a random passage to read out, like a genie magicking him into the room with us. I traced the glossy cover with my fingertips and thought how lovely it was to have a relationship with another writer. My parents had both been writers when they met, but they never talked of it with any romance. They always maintained that one person should have a proper job, and that somehow they had landed up together. They had both stopped writing at exactly the same time, when they came to England, and both taken up proper jobs. I thought about living in a cramped apartment filled with the sounds of typing and wastepaper bins overflowing with trashed manuscripts. I thought of smoking relentless cigarettes and ice cubes smashing against whiskey glasses and coffee bubbling on the hob. Being naked together and writing furiously through the night and making love at dawn. I stared at the pages with dissatisfaction. I was no writer, I had no agent any more and the little manuscript that I'd knocked up in three months lay inertly on the breakfast hatch, collecting dust.

I threw myself into the time when he had written his book, he hadn't known me then and I was jealous. I looked again for a dedication and decided he couldn't have loved anyone ever if he hadn't dedicated his book to them. I flicked through, looking for clues, but it wasn't that sort of book. It was a series of analytical essays on various Black and Asian characters in classic literature. It was very highbrow and dense, with large footnotes covering the pages and it reminded me of those photocopies that I'd never bothered to read and had used to line my underwear drawers. I skimmed through the book impatiently – I'd never even heard of any of the characters. Finally, I found something I recognized.

'Listen to this,' I said triumphantly, 'Othello was bound to kill Desdemona because every man destroys the thing he loves. Else, it destroys him.'

'Sounds boring,' said Frank. 'What do you want me to say, that it's profound? So that you can have another reason to love him?'

'You don't read books, you don't know what you're on about,' I said.

'Alright, but what does this man know about love? He's had one failed marriage, he's got two women with whom he's had kids and he's still running around trying to prove what a man he is. I don't think that's very mature. It's irresponsible. How could Othello have known that Desdemona would have left him? Only if he was insecure.'

We did it for A level, that play. Did Othello love wisely or too well? No one knew, we were all seventeen, we got the answer out of the *Key Facts*. We went to see the film and gave the teacher a nervous breakdown by smoking and snogging in the back row. What were your impressions, class? Why did his make-up come off on Desdemona, sir? Looked like the black and white minstrels, sir.

The next day, Frank and I both opened our eyes at the same time, listening to the deep stillness outside, not a bird, not a voice.

'I like it here . . . ' I started to say, staring at the ceiling, rigid.

'It's really quiet . . . ' said Frank, staring at the ceiling, rigid.

We both sat bolt upright.

'Let's get out of here,' we both screamed.

'We'll hire a car and go to Madrid,' he said.

'I'll kill myself if I have to spend my New Year's with a load of geriatrics,' I said.

'There's no one here under fifty,' said Frank in dismay.

We looked at each other in panic. We decided to go out for breakfast, and after that straight to the Car Hire. Madrid would be happening, and we had friends there who would know of wild parties.

By the time we got our act together, it was siesta time and all the shops were closed. We stomped down to the beach café in a bad mood, and ordered breakfast while others were well into their lunch, dressed in towelling robes over swimwear. It was warmer and the sea was shimmering endlessly. Birds flew in straight lines overhead in the blue brilliant sky. The pipe woman and her companion were in exactly the same place, mesmerized by each other's conversation, eating salads in slow motion. We stared at them dumbly.

'We're not doing this right,' mumbled Frank.

'It's not that bad here,' I said.

'We can't go to Madrid,' said Frank. 'That's like still being in London mode rushing about. We're with each other, that's enough. Let's relax. Let's take time out to make decisions about the new year.'

On the night before New Year's Eve, I couldn't sleep. I sat down in the bathroom and pressed my face against the cool tiles. I knew the next year was coming and the next and I would have to go on with the business of living. I wrote a letter to Amrit.

Dear Amrit,
I've been thinking about everything on holiday. You are probably the most interesting man I have ever met and I'm filled with excitement at the thought of you. But all I would ever be is a part of your semi-detached life and I'm not used to that. I wouldn't be able to handle it. I hope you will always be my friend.

*

'Keep it for four days,' said Frank. 'Never send a letter to a lover on the spur of the moment.'

The idea of Amrit being referred to as my lover sent a thrill through me. The next evening, we opened a bottle of Cava. We weren't on the beach, we were inside a restaurant with people carousing and singing. There was a dance band playing old hits and the songs were all in Spanish, everything decorated with coloured bulbs and streamers, the women's eyes shining, hot garlicky smoke buffeting out of the kitchen. They started doing a countdown.

'Make a copy,' advised Frank.

I felt very clever, on top of things. The future full of hope and possibilities, just the way everyone feels at all New Year parties when they're very young. Those little victories. I have to deal with the rest of it, the rest of the debris, but I am happy now, in this moment, because I have acted and my burden is less, and there is room to be happy. We had felt that way, Luke and I, hadn't we? We hadn't made a scene, we had accepted the ending, laughed over cigarettes. It all seemed so far away. We were equals, we were friends; I hadn't really loved Luke.

'Can't do that,' I laughed, 'like a memo.'

The sky was awash with brilliant explosions. I wanted to feel very brave and noble as young lovers are supposed to feel. I wanted to feel the feeling explode like a firecracker and then die majestically, watch the lights fade out against the night sky, emerge intact, rejuvenated by the sight of it, by the death of it. But already the moment had gone, there was no room left. Suddenly there was only darkness.

'I hope you make all the right decisions for yourself in the New Year,' said Frank and hugged me.

I held on tight and I wanted to cry because I knew I was making the biggest mistake of my life and I couldn't forgive myself.

'Let's drink to friendship,' I said.

'Let's sail without a plan,' said Frank. 'I like that, do you think it would be alright to steal it? That's what I'm going to say to my lovers. It's got a nice ring to it.'

'I'll give him the letter. I'll face him out. And then I'll never see him again. It's too dangerous. I can't even imagine what kinds of damage it'll do to me.'

'Better to find someone who's not so charismatic, not so powerful. Just someone who loves you,' said Frank, 'so you can get on with the rest of your life.'

CHAPTER TWELVE

I couldn't remember a time after that holiday in Spain when I was really happy. It seems a strange claim to make for a period in a life. So many wonderful things happened to me, but there was a dull ache all the time, a knowledge of defeat in my bones, a proliferation of shame. Loving Amrit was a Sisyphean task. There was no meaning or reward in it, and yet it grew in me, the more distant he became. The first time I noticed the distance close up was after I slept with him.

I left it a week before phoning him, let the New Year wash over me. I found a job. In the Holloway Road was a large old-fashioned department store called Jones Brothers and they were looking for temporary staff during the January sales. I was assigned to the gloves and hats section under the tutelage of Mrs Menozzi, an old dragon with ironed hair and an erect back. She looked like a headmistress and disapproved of the store hiring inexperienced young people at a time when all the permanent jobs were at risk. Rumour had it that Jones Brothers was not competitive enough and private developers had earmarked the site for a supermarket. In the back of the gloves and hats section was a little kitchenette where breathless gossip was exchanged between Mrs Menozzi and her colleagues from Menswear and Gardening Tools.

It was one of those stores that still had large oak staircases instead of escalators. They stocked half sizes in leather gloves, undertook minor alterations free of charge, gift wrapped the smallest item on request. They had a system of payment which would have rivalled any store in Moscow. It involved getting a receipt for a purchase, and then queuing up to get the goods on presentation of the receipt. It was possible to spend the best part of a day in Jones Brothers just buying a few items. There were several of us graduates sprinkled around the store. Other than polite nods, none of us bothered to make friends with each other. We had a life outside work for chrissakes! For us it was a stop gap, a way of earning a bit of cash and we sniggered at the older members of staff who took such care and pride over how to fold a garment or arrange the gloves in their boxes. A guy called Connor worked upstairs in Menswear and we had often arrived late and rushed up the stairs together. Although he arrived for work in full motorbike leathers, I had smiled to see him in the canteen, by the window, in his dreary grey suit, reading *The Irish Times*.

The work was part-time which suited me very well. I didn't want to think I'd completely sold out and started working for a living. Frank gave me his old ansaphone as a present to commiserate with my first week in the world of work. He had bought himself the latest Panasonic cordless ansaphone and fax in one. Now, he said, we could leave long rambling messages for each other without any interruptions.

It was a cold January day when I phoned Amrit, my palms wet against the telephone.

'You waited a week,' he said in dismay.

I thought I would go for lunch and be nonchalant, but when I arrived in the restaurant and saw him at the far table watching the door anxiously, all the monsters in my mind evaporated, my heart soared, I was unaware of anyone else. In the large mirror, I saw the flash of my short black skirt, the gleam of my hair. How gorgeous I looked, how proud; I had never seen myself looking so lucky. It was unbelievable that he was really sitting in a restaurant, awaiting my company. We didn't bore each other, speak of how the holiday was, my new job, his complicated life, all the stuff of conversation between people who had time to kill. We drank too much wine and stared at each other like lovers.

In his car after lunch, he asked me casually if I had read any good books recently. I had been dreading this question. To my shame, I had speed-read, nervously gleaning the text for his experience, afraid of women's names. The politics and highbrow ideas had passed me by.

'What sort of people do you suppose read that kind of book,' I said, 'for pleasure, I mean?' I hadn't meant it as a slight, in fact always felt intimidated by my fellow students who sailed through large ponderous books, even discussed them animatedly in the Union bar.

'Well, not too many,' smiled Amrit. 'I don't sell terribly well, you know. But the publishers keep asking me and they give me some lolly, so I continue. It's also part of the job, you know. Academia isn't about teaching really, it's about research and publication.'

'You must have read a hundred books. You must be really well read,' I said enviously.

'I suppose I must be,' he said deflated. 'Is there anything you liked about it?'

'You,' I said cheerfully, 'I liked that it was written by you.'

He laughed and squeezed my hand, told me I was harsh and exacting and full of guts. We talked incessantly as he drove me home, fragmented conversations that made me think we were friends, because friends did not have to patronize each other, friends could love endlessly. He stopped the car outside my flat staring at the steering wheel.

'Hey,' I said, after he had remained in the same position for seconds.

'I feel as though I'm in a trance,' he said in a grave voice. I laughed. I didn't know what to say.

'I can't abandon everything. I just can't abandon everything.' The words were like an incantation. I looked outside the window at my path and my trees and everything which was nothing to do with him, would never be. The silence in the car was thick, like paint.

'I suppose a shag's out of the question then?' I said poker-faced.

He burst out laughing. I wanted to make him laugh, bring everything out in the open and keep it secret too. I had a feeling suddenly, that love must not be talked of too much, or else it would degenerate into hearts and flowers and valentine cards. He revved the motor and I went to open the car door.

'Keep yourself with care,' he said gently in Hindi, putting his hand on mine.

In the early months of the year, cold and wet, we met frequently and had lunch or he would come to my flat for a few hours and we would talk. I burning with desire, he sedate. I told him about Mrs Menozzi who had started a petition against the proposed sale of the huge store where she and many of the others had worked since they were in their twenties, ex-students like us. The idea of working in a job for that long was shocking to me, and then to fight a losing battle for keeping that job, ludicrous. I felt sorry for them fighting against the wind of inevitability. I giggled and told Amrit that the work was a doddle, it was great to have some cash to supplement the meagre allowance that RaviKavi were forking out. He looked at me keenly, held my hand as I chattered away. There was never any compulsion on his part as far as I could see. He was conducting a strange courtship of neglect. It fascinated me.

While I was always expecting him to provoke my submission, he did nothing. He never mentioned making love or baby doll or getting inside the middle of me. He behaved in exactly the same way as he had done before we'd kissed:

courteous, benign, in for the long haul. He would phone me and say, 'May I see you?' and then leave after kissing me at the door, saying he would see me soon. Weeks would pass and I would hear no more from him, until I phoned, rattling the cage to see if it was dead, yet feverishly hoping that the thing had died in me without trouble. But he would answer my calls excitedly as though we were long lost dear friends, and again the excitement would revive and burst into flames inside me.

I knew there was a sell-by date, knew that this time was a lead up, knew things would change once we had gone to bed. I wanted to use this time properly, utilize it. Dig my feet into the ground, get an overview, make assessments, free of the confusions that having sex with him would undoubtedly create, but I couldn't manage it. I was falling in love anyway, as he had predicted, and although I watched myself fretfully, hoping for signs of normal living, I was completely lost.

He would call me from one of his homes, he called them houses, to tell me about an article he had read, or take up a conversation we had broken off days ago. We spoke in a mixture of Hindi and English and IndianEnglish, making silly jokes with words. I would gasp if he used a swear word, even an innocuous one, because I had never heard the words fuck and sister fucker and bastard in translation. I had thought Indians to be a polite, clean-living, rather dull race. He would snicker at my outrage.

'We're friends,' he said one day, 'we understand each other. Yet you still use "aap", you still use the formal with me.'

'I respect you,' I said, 'I love you and I respect you.'

He stared at me and looked away. And then in some perverse bid to flatten my faith in him, he said, 'Do you know what some of Ralph's friends used to call Matty?'

'What?' I said, disorientated by the way he always veered the subject away.

'They used to call her doormatty.'

I stared at him. I felt like crying.

'I didn't call her that,' he said.

*

The feeling of love was not the same as the feeling of life. I felt alive when I was with him, but I didn't feel I was living. Living was the consolidation of ordinary acts – shopping for food, talking to friends on the phone, reading a book slowly, wandering aimlessly on a rare sunny day, cleaning the kitchen floor, selling gloves. With Amrit, I felt alert, guarded, listening keenly, turning around the feeling in front of the lightbulb of reason, wondering what kind of love felt such deep fear. I spent days thinking about him and how he would push himself on me, devastated by the finality of it. It was like driving towards a dead end without brakes. Occasionally, he would make comments that shattered my storehouse of knowledge.

It was Spring, the skeleton trees outside my flat had grown little buds and the sky was pale, the breeze swelled against watery sunshine. Jones Brothers had asked me and some other sales staff to stay on. Connor and I had afternoon coffee together sometimes. He was a Union man and was helping Mrs Menozzi to organize her fellow workers. My job had changed. I had been put in charge of the back stock in the basement. There was a huge amount of stock to be catalogued, crated, categorized. Their filing system was Dickensian. I felt myself transported in time while I was at work, snuggled inside the basement with reams of paper, ticking off items, sure of everything. Outside, I was sure of nothing, suspended in pure anticipation.

I made Amrit walk with me to the 24-hour petrol station to get cigarettes one evening, cutting into those precious three or four hours that he took off from his real life to come and sit in my front room with the coffee table. He pointed to the nursery school on that road and casually said, 'Our child might go there, it would be so convenient.'

'What did you say?' I said, jerking my head.

He laughed and turned away. I felt as though he was embarrassed by how easy it was to trip me with words, make me believe things by a throw-away phrase. Sometimes I would ask him why he said such things, things he couldn't possibly mean. He would say don't worry, things will iron themselves out. At the time it seemed to me that he was being ambiguous, afraid to say what was really in his heart, hiding behind words. Later, I realized that there were different lines for different girls.

What we take to be chemistry between lovers has been analyzed sometimes as the mirror one shows to the other. In the mirror of the beloved we see ourselves grow and develop. Amrit was like Dr Livingstone, showing me magic mirrors and hiding them away before I could get a closer look, leaving me with my burgeoning imagination. Love for him was an act of control, not just controlling the object of love, but controlling his own giving, withholding himself. I had a distinct feeling that he believed he would die if he stripped himself of his armour. It was as compelling as any number of baubles and mirrors must have been to natives in the jungle. I used to think I must be like a guerrilla, edging into his terrain, turning the mirror back to him. And then seeing himself, he would give in, let himself be claimed like a convert. Believe in everything he didn't believe in.

Up till the time I slept with him there was a foothold, the luxury of such fantasies that I sustained myself with. He arrived one chilly March evening in a state of high excitement and I was eager to share his mood. He said he had escaped.

'Clarissa started her first job today,' he said. 'After ten years of looking after the kid, she's finally decided to work for a living like the rest of us.'

'Isn't looking after kids a . . . ' I didn't bother to finish my sentence. It was between them.

'I bought her a bottle of champagne, had one glass and said I'm off.'

'Didn't she mind?' I said curiously.

'She thinks I am a fraud,' he said and laughed.

There was a whole relationship in those words. I was shaking with disbelief, at his easy manner, at all he was hiding from me.

'Then I phoned Jonesy from a phone box and said I was going to a party, and then I came to you.'

'Why don't you take her to the party?'

'One doesn't go to parties with wives, one goes to parties with girlfriends.'

There was always a terrifying formality in his conversations. He never had rambling open-ended conversations the way people do; he spoke in hard sentences, factual reportage, as though a proper conversation was wet and flabby. As though communication between two people was something to get over and done with. I felt always as though I must be on my toes, answer in an equally sharp way. Detail, nuance, musing, chit chat made his eyes glaze over. I was afraid that his interest would wane if I took too long in responding. I had the feeling that he must have had so many conversations along the same lines with so many women, that they bored him, the simple conversations between men and women.

'I'm not your girlfriend.'

'You're the love of my life.'

'For now.'

'How do you know?'

'Because you don't care about things.'

'I was brought up just like you. I am good and honest and truthful. A decent man. An example to young persons like yourself,' he said mockingly.

'Oh really,' I said sourly.

'It's not what you think. Those relationships are stale. I sleep in my own room. I share the business of the kids. You have no idea. You're free and young and you're going to be a great writer. Your parents were poets, I had to overcome so much to be a writer.'

'Am I supposed to feel sorry for you?'

'I know you feel nothing but contempt for me,' he said evenly.

'Relationships don't go stale like fish. They end,' I said angrily.

'I can't abandon things, there are obligations I must keep.'

'How can you behave like this? What must they think of you? You must have loved them to have children with them?'

'These things happen. Love? I don't know, I suppose a kind of love. Sometimes I think that Clarissa is like a cat and Jonesy is like a dog.'

'What did you say?' I stared at him incredulously.

'Clarissa doesn't want anything to do with me. She wants to be left alone. She wants only for me to pay the bills and sign the house over to her. And Jonesy clings.'

Cats and dogs and doormats and the crease on a trouser. This was how he saw women, this man that I was deciding to make love with. I was editing his words as he spoke, remembering only that he thought I was to be a great writer.

'What makes you say I feel nothing but contempt for you?' I said.

'It's your way of loving me.'

'What a horrible thing to say.' I was devastated.

'I'm afraid,' he said, and stared at me so hard I giggled.

'You should be,' I said narrowing my eyes. 'Be very afraid.'

He laughed out loud. I was looking at my manuscript on the breakfast hatch. It was the copy that Torquil had sent to me along with a letter listing publishers he was going to try. Reams of paper sitting on the hatch, so small in that room filled with his laughter.

'I was wondering,' he said, suddenly serious, catching my gaze, 'when you were going to let me read your book.'

'I'm sure you're far too busy to read it,' I said.

'Far too busy.' He walked across and picked up the manuscript with both hands and placed it carefully inside his bag. He looked over at me, as if to say, try and stop me.

'I don't think it will ever get published,' I grumbled, hoping in some oblique way we would have a conversation where he would reassure me that getting published was a mere formality, the way all my friends had. He sat down next to me and took my hand in his.

'Will you do me the honour of accompanying me to this party, so I can stand next to you and show everybody I know someone remarkable?'

'Is that the all-purpose line? With the girls, I mean.'

'It's what I think,' he said, 'and you can fuck off if you don't believe me.'

It was some sort of charity thing at the university. We danced in full view of everyone; I was laughing when he did some version of the twist.

'I really like you,' he said. 'I really do. We're into something.'

We came back from the party and he had a condom with him. The way he was concentrating on extracting it from the packet, it was obvious he hadn't handled one for years, if ever. He's so old, I thought.

It was a clumsy affair. He said afterwards that he must leave, because people would be worried about him, wondering where he had pitched up in the middle of the night. He always referred to them as people, as though they were nameless, objective strangers, those women who were the mothers of his children. And I thought, for this you held me at arms' length. For this you encouraged my intrigue. Not even to lie in my arms afterwards and think the world softer and good. All your plans laid so that you could prowl out in the middle of the night holding your shoes in your hand. It wasn't done, even he knew that, so he stayed the night. He was begrudging, it was as though I had asked an unreasonable thing. We lay silently. In the morning he didn't kiss me and instead went about the business of showering as though he were in a dormitory. He knew, he must have known, there were things one had to do to get it over, the passion, but maybe he had done them so often that they were tiresome, the things that women expected. I thought it was different when you loved someone, however many times you loved someone. I didn't think you could grow weary of loving.

He walked with me in the spitting morning. We walked and walked along the Holloway Road without an umbrella, and I waited with every step for him to say something, but he didn't say anything. We just trudged along in the fragile rain. It's finished for him, I was thinking, and it's beginning for me. When we neared the store, I told him to go in case anyone saw him. It would look strange to people. Someone like him, walking in the rain with me in the early morning.

He said, 'I was writing you a letter, but I never sent it.'

I remembered the letter I had written in Spain, which I had never sent, never looked at again. It was lying in a drawer.

'Why didn't you send it?' I asked.

'I didn't know how to say things,' he said, 'say the feelings I feel.'

I wondered if it would have been better if he had sent me a letter, words in ink scrawled upon Basildon Bond. Later, I lost the conviction that he had ever written such a letter, I believed it to be some kind of device to fill the silence between us. But then, that morning in the rain, still hopeful, I rejoiced that he had tried to do something for me.

'Couldn't you bear to kiss me?' I said.

He looked at me strangely and said he never did that. He just got up every morning and got ready for work and got in his car.

'Why are you lying to me? I'm late for work, I'm really late,' I cried, my eyes full of tears that I had held back along the long grey Holloway Road.

'I have a sinus thing,' he said. 'My nose is all bunged up in the morning. I've had it since I was a child. It used to make me miserable.'

Afterwards, drinking coffee, swallowing bile, the smart of humiliation on my face, I thought why hadn't I changed the situation? Why hadn't I laughed when he couldn't keep his erection, when he could only do it for moments? I wondered why I had not exacted my revenge and now it was too late. I slipped out of the basement to phone Frank from the pay phone along the corridor, looking over my shoulder because staff weren't supposed to use the phones other than at lunchtime.

'He didn't even kiss me. He must hate my guts.'

'You're over-reacting,' said Frank.

'I started crying outside the bloody store.'

'You must have frightened the life out of him. My grandma's got sinus problems, they fuck up your nose. He'll phone you and everything will be alright.'

Frank didn't know anything. I knew Amrit wouldn't phone. Frank thought he was just a man in a mid-life crisis, who was dazzled by a young attractive girl. It was too simple an explanation for me. I couldn't allow Amrit to be mundane in my eyes, it would have detracted from my fascination for him, made me mundane by association. After all, I had almost died to get to him.

By the end of the day, having replayed events in my mind, tired from their clarity, I went back on every paranoid thought and turned it into a list of reasons to be hopeful. Men had egos, I was young, he was old, people had sinuses, not everyone expressed every emotion as soon as they had it. I'm not doing this right, I told myself the way Frank and I had told each other at the beach café. As soon as it was six o'clock, I raced out to the street and flung myself into a phone box. I punched out his number – Clarissa's number, because that was where he 'stayed' most often, that was where there was less trouble as he called it. I was ready to say sweet things into the phone, behave as clandestine lovers behave. He said he was cooking a meal, he would phone me later. Distressed, I went to see a movie by myself, full of car crashes and loud music, and let the tears fall down my cheeks. When I got home and rushed to check my ansaphone, there were no messages.

CHAPTER THIRTEEN

'Hi, it's me.'

'Hello?' I said uncertainly into the phone.

I had waited for five days and Amrit had not phoned me. I had gone over everything that had happened between us. I couldn't make head nor tail of it. Even adolescents knew it wasn't done to not phone or make contact the day after you had slept with a girl. It was monstrous of him.

'Hellooo,' cooed Luke.

'Luke! Oh god, Luke!' I said. 'When did you get back?'

'A few days ago. I tried you earlier but you've got one of those stupid things. How are you?'

'Let's meet, Luke. Come over,' I pleaded.

Luke had been away for over six months and I sat watching TV as I waited for him. Whenever Amrit visited me, even when there were only days in between meetings, I would hang out of the window watching the empty street, making bets that the next car around the corner would be his. The bell rang.

'You look great,' I said.

We hugged each other at the door. He sat down on the

sofa looking around at the transformation of the flat. Last time it had been an empty shell, full of anonymous crates, where we'd sit on the floor and eat takeaways out of foil containers. He had grown thinner and his skin had coloured slightly as if he'd been running. He looked older.

We had a bottle of wine and he told me about his travels. I watched how animated he was, his hands moving around. The criterion of the international artists' colony, was that each resident's research must involve India in some way. He had met musicians and artists and actors from Japan and Vietnam and Peru. They had exchanged ideas and invited each other to workshops. The ideology of the artists' colony was that everybody should also participate in the domestic chores, like devotees in an ashram, so that an artist's life did not become an abstract concept. Yoga was practised in the mornings, light meals provided in the afternoons, problems of diminished gas and electricity and milk were dealt with by the artists themselves. However, the nightlife had been hectic, and decadent, mixing with the Delhi élite. They had gone to jazz bars and embassy parties, rubbed shoulders with ambassadors, fashion designers, politicians and socialites. I felt a little aggrieved that Luke had accessed a society that I didn't even know existed.

'India is so fascinating,' he said. 'So urbane yet almost medieval. There are so many contradictions. Position matters so much. Hierarchy is everything. People hold court, demolish someone's status and credibility in public. Rewards given, favours taken. Obligation is all.'

'Aren't all societies like that?' I said, mildly perturbed that he seemed to know India better than I.

'I felt such an Englishman. I was given privileges because I was from England. And I'm not talking about in villages, this is amongst sophisticated urbanites. I felt like I was someone important, when I'm not at all. I can't deny I liked it though.' He smiled apologetically. 'Anyway, enough about me, tell me how you've been?'

I looked away and sipped my wine. I was working in a

stupid department store, I had written an idiotic novel which was rotting somewhere unpublished, and I had fallen for someone who didn't give a damn about me. I felt my eyes stinging with tears.

'Everything's gone wrong, Luke. I don't know what I'm doing any more.'

'What's happened?' he said with concern.

'I've started seeing Amrit,' I said looking at the floor.

Luke didn't speak for moments. Then he sighed. 'I thought something like that might happen.'

I was glad I'd told Luke. It wasn't to do with guilt, I didn't feel any. It was to do with my need to know he was still my friend in the face of the worst storm.

'There's no substance to him, you know,' said Luke bitterly. 'He doesn't care about anything.'

He was hurt, I had hurt him, I hadn't thought. A wave of tiredness crashed through me.

'But it doesn't work like that,' I said. 'Love doesn't work that way.'

Luke poured out the wine and we looked at each other. 'Are you in love with him?'

'I don't know if it's love, it's a kind of infatuation that feels like love. I don't know where I am with him. I don't know what I mean to him. I can't stop thinking about it. Luke, I'm sorry.'

Luke shrugged and sipped his wine. 'You have to suffer,' he said. 'That's how it is.'

He got up and stared out of the window at the weak sunlight filtering through the trees. 'Was it going on when we went to the party?' he said tightly.

'No, Luke. No,' I said tearfully. 'Not till much later. It's nothing like...It's different.' I raised my hand helplessly, an impotent gesture.

Luke turned around and walked back to the sofa. 'There's something you should know,' he said carefully.

'I know,' I said, 'Matty. Actually, she told me about it. I didn't know it at the time, but she was telling me about it.'

Luke's face was set in hard lines. It was the same expression I had seen on his face when Amrit had congratulated him on his grant. A kind of controlled hopelessness.

'Ralph was the first man she'd ever known. Matty's from a really straight family. Vicar's daughter and all that. She thought it was all for ever. Then he walked out on us and moved in with that girl. It made her feel old and ugly, thrown away. She turned to me. The girls were too young to understand. I had to be strong. We used to read and talk together. I couldn't bear her to be so lonely. I knew she thought she'd missed out on life. I used to tell her she'd meet someone else, she didn't need Ralph. She'd meet someone who would treat her as she ought to be treated.' He sighed and shook his head. 'Then Amrit started coming round. He used to turn up whenever, just turn up and crash on the settee. He made her laugh, she thought he was interesting and gentle and he listened to her. I suppose he made her feel attractive.'

I was listening fiercely. I knew Luke was telling me intimate details and that I should have felt for Matty, but all I was interested in was Amrit, how he had seduced her, had it been different, better with me, was I just another woman of no consequence. It horrified me, the way Matty had passed out of the fold of my generosity, everyone had, anyone who presented a threat to my getting closer to Amrit. It was dangerous. It was obsessive.

'How long did it last?' I asked nervously.

Luke looked at me with pity and held my stare. 'Not long. It never does with him.'

He's so angry with me, I was thinking. He wants so much to denounce me from his heart for my callousness. How far apart I've torn us. When Luke left he said that he was back in the squat and that I could call him sometime, though not yet, not for a while yet. I understood. He knew I no longer belonged to him. I'm alone, I thought with terror, everything's breaking away. I couldn't bring myself to call Amrit. Things were different now, I felt like an interloper, like a caricature, a woman on a television programme railing against betrayal.

'It's only a week,' said Frank, 'only one week. Don't be so unreasonable. You expect too much. Don't be so involved. He's afraid, isn't that what he told you?'

But I was convinced about love; it won't let you wait as the song said. If he wanted me he wouldn't hesitate. And the thought of all those other women, past and present, crowding up his life made me feel small, so small that I would stare at shop windows to make sure I was still there. I smarted at my foolishness, wondered how I could be so adolescent in my understanding of this game. People slept with each other and took phone numbers and said all sorts of things to people they never saw again. I had done it myself, but all at once, I couldn't remember my past, I couldn't draw on any single experience I had undergone. I had become a child staring at the world of grown-ups, devoid of guile and knowing, convinced of my mortality. I was nearly twenty-five years old, nearly a quarter of a century into my life. When would I grow up and know everything?

Once, as a child, I had been watching my dad fix a lampshade when the phone rang and he went to answer it in the hallway. 'Don't touch anything,' he said. As soon as I had heard him open a conversation in Hindi, knowing it would evolve into a spiralling dialogue, unlike his stilted English phone calls with insurance companies or bank tellers, I stuck my finger into the socket of the lamp where the bulb was supposed to go. The shock rammed through me like a rocket, and I tore my hand away, shaking from head to foot, convinced I had died. I was sitting on my hand when my dad returned and went back to his work. I sat very still, my eyes shining, my heart beating, but he couldn't tell. I realized with a quiet satisfaction that the electricity that had surged through my body had left no tell-tale signs. I thought, with a quiet superiority, that I was capable of upturning a law of physics.

In the middle of the night, the phone rang.

The week had drawn to a close and I was convinced I would never see Amrit again. I lurched awake, full of trepidation. A phone call at this time could only mean that one of my parents was dangerously ill. I had developed this sixth sense of foreboding that all lone children carry at the back of their heart, this running thread of fear that one of the points of the triangle will fall down and collapse the whole structure. I dreaded international calls.

'I'm in Paris. I'm writing you a letter, I wish you were beside me,' said Amrit. 'I'm sorry to phone you at this hour. Forgive me.'

Relief flooded through my blood, turning to a high excitement, as his voice growled in my ear, in my cold, still, dark bedroom. He said he'd been invited to a conference. He was staying in a fancy hotel at their expense. Excitement and jealousy braided themselves together inside me. The stab of jealousy, that while I had lain awake every night trying to make sense of that uneventful night, he had carried on living.

In an urgent whisper, as though he were telling me a codeword, he said he was in love with me. 'If we ran away together, then everything would be devastated. Families, reputations, what would I say to your father?'

I listened to his words in the cold. I was afraid of the things he was saying, of the effect they were having on me. I was thinking of Paris and how wonderful to be there and order room service.

'You don't know what you are,' he said.

'Why are you saying these things?' I said desperately. 'Why are you trying to deceive me?'

He turned up at Jones Brothers a week later. He came into the hats and gloves department and asked Mrs Menozzi politely if he may have a word with me. My colleagues looked at each other when I emerged from the basement. In the corridor, he gave me a pack of duty free cigarettes, he'd just come from the airport. Delirious at this spontaneous gesture, my heart leaping at the sight of his smiling face and at the same time terrified of what the others were thinking, I clutched his sleeve.

'What did you mean on the phone?' I said urgently. 'Did you mean what you said?' I had thought of nothing else, the phone call from Paris had festered inside me all week.

'I've double-parked the car,' he said, 'I'll call you.'

I cried all the way home on the bus and felt dirty and useless. I told myself it was a regular thing that men did, made drunken phone calls from Paris about love and running away. Modern girls were supposed to know it was all chat, all part of the game. Modern girls weren't supposed to take it seriously. He didn't call me, so I called him the next day. He wasn't available every time I called and I wondered if he had told his secretary to divert my calls. I stared at the carton of cigarettes. They were the pay off. I felt a hurricane of rage that he hadn't even bothered with perfume or underwear or scarves. He doesn't even rate you as a high-class whore.

The letter arrived two days later. He had waited till the last minute to post it. I thought it would be a lover's letter, a flamboyant over-blown symphony to love, but it was little more than a memo. He wondered why I wasn't in Paris; I didn't know what a beauty I was; the scene outside his window. I was crushed. There was no mention of love, nothing that could be used in evidence against him. I read it over and over and folded it back into its envelope. He was a writer, the letter was inexcusable. Writers wrote expressive love letters, I had heard. He can't write letters like that any more, I thought suddenly. But he wrote them once. He must have written them once. It only happens once. One only marries once. It came to me on a rainy morning on top of a crowded bus. It's already happened to him, years ago, the lightning, it's burnt him through. It only happens once. The realization froze me rigid.

I felt desperate, couldn't concentrate at work. Mrs Menozzi and her conspirators had become vocal. They were openly talking of confrontation, of trade unions and unfair dismissal, these old people who were at the end of their lives. Mrs Menozzi walked erect in her court shoes, up and down the side of the counter, her mouth pursing with outrage at every new edict that dropped from the management. Certain lines were discontinued; various sections were to be closed; overtime was eliminated. I felt the minutes ticking by. I must speak to him. I slipped away from Mrs Menozzi's hawk-like gaze and phoned him three times at the university, hating the secretary's smarmy voice. The fourth time, he took the call himself and said he was deluged with work. I slammed the phone down.

What's happening to me, I thought. What's happening to me?

He came to my flat that night, sat in my front room and said we would have to have some rules. He looked at me doubtfully, as though he knew it was useless asking me to behave within protocol.

'You must be joking,' I snorted. 'Is that the kind of shit that passes for a relationship with white women?'

'It's nothing to do with that. You can't get so angry whenever I can't speak to you. It's not always possible for me.'

'What happened to sailing without plans?' I said triumphantly.

'I'm getting too involved with you.'

'Isn't that good?' I said, my eyes shining.

'No,' he said and laughed. 'It's very bad.'

And with this slight conversation, he seemed to have made a decision. The decision to retreat.

'I don't believe you,' I said.

'Love has to develop, it must have somewhere to go. There's nowhere I can take you. It's on my mind constantly. I feel ridiculous. I can't continue with this,' he said gently. 'It's not good for you.'

'Of course you can,' I said, full of confidence, buoyed up by his words of love. 'You must. You can't bury things.'

'Then you must be nice.'

Nice meant I should not love so hard. Nice meant that I should not take him seriously. Nice meant that I should think of him as someone dispensable.

'You must think of me as some guy who's around. When he's here it's fun and when he's not here it doesn't matter,' he said.

Because it didn't hurt yet, because nothing was broken inside yet, I was amused by his idea of relationships, by the way he planned his emotions. It was not a strategy I had come across previously, that someone should turn away at the point of loving. It seemed to me absurd and transitory at the time, words spoken in bravado. It seemed to me an overt challenge, a throwing down of the gauntlet in the middle of a war. It was too ridiculous to take seriously, like a child saying he was afraid of the dark. I took it upon myself to lead him through the night, I who had upturned a law of physics. He tried to remove himself from loving, but I made it impossible, by being so pleased at the sound of his voice, by teasing him about his stuffiness, until finally he gave in.

He started staying later than he should. He would phone me three times a day and reprimand me for leaving my ansaphone on. Further than that he did not dare. I had seen movies and read novels where people had wild affairs, I knew what they did. They stole time away together. When I hinted at day trips, weekends, holidays, he said it was not possible.

'But, you've done those things with other women. You don't care about telling lies,' I protested, eager to get the full value of having an affair with an older man who knew about wines and had more money than I.

'If I go somewhere with you, I won't be able to come back,' he said.

Perhaps he was hoping for a natural death, hoping it would dwindle away like his previous countless affairs. What are you doing with a decrepit old man like me any way, he'd say and I, refusing to fuel his vanity, would retort that it was a mercy mission. He seemed to enjoy those conversations, when he could cast me as a wild unpredictable thing who was simply passing the time with him, picking up an interesting pebble on the shore before throwing it back.

'You're going to have a wonderful life,' he said, looking seriously into my eyes, 'and I'll say, I knew her. I loved her and she never found out.'

Summer hit London again in a big way. There was a heatwave and all the pubs in town were heaving with people in shorts and girls in skimpy dresses. The foliage grew thick and unwieldy outside my window; strange birds appeared. Invitations to parties and barbecues fell on my mat and I threw them in the bin. Frank told me I was a fool. I didn't care, I was full of happiness, I didn't care how long it lasted. Tash sent me a few postcards all at once, like a conversation strung out on paper. How's the coffin dodger, she wrote.

Amrit took to phoning me daily, at night, from one of the houses, in a bid I presumed, to show me he slept in his own room. We talked for hours, listening to each other's voice. I lay in bed and wondered if I had dreamed the conversation, dreamed his gentleness, the sadness in his voice, those desperate declarations. And then, in the light of day, like his retort about the car being double-parked, he would behave as though he had never said those things, as though we were just friends.

'You're like the fucking Chancellor of the Exchequer,' I said to him, 'putting a pond in my pocket and taking it away in VAT.' He laughed at my imitation of an Indian, saying pond instead of pound.

When he came to the flat, often he would refuse to come to my bedroom, insisting that he had a story to tell me, or just that he wanted to sit at the coffee table and drink wine and talk with me. I didn't know whether to be flattered or dismayed.

On the first of June I failed my driving test. He said he would take me out to commiserate and where did I want to go. I immediately named an expensive restaurant. Because he went to expensive restaurants all the time, as did the people he moved with, he didn't understand my fascination with them. RaviKavi had never been to a restaurant in their lives out of choice. My dad couldn't see the point of wasting good money on bad food. As far as he was concerned, my mum was the best cook in the world, he the second best. Obviously, a non-Indian restaurant was not even worthy of consideration. Consequently, I had reached adulthood with an unnatural fascination for eating out, a ritual I practised as often as I could. Amrit said, no, he didn't want to go to that restaurant. I slammed the phone down, thinking he didn't want to spend so much money on me. He called back, his voice was tired, he was trying to be nice.

'I didn't want to take you there, because I know the woman who runs it and she'll gossip about you. She'll say Amrit was here with this woman and so on and so forth.'

I shouted that it hadn't stopped him from taking other women, white women. He had taken Matty to a hotel in London, what was so wonderful about her?

'It was different with them, it was different.'

'They were worthy of it,' I retorted with outrage. 'That's what you mean. They were worthy of being wined and dined.'

'They needed it. They required it,' he said.

'I need it too,' I shouted.

'You don't need trivial things like that. You have higher concerns.'

'Don't talk bullshit,' my voice wavered into the telephone.

He sighed and said, 'Alright, we'll go, I want to do whatever you want.'

Hearing the pull in his voice, the gulf I had hacked between us, I admitted that I didn't care if we had a takeaway, I just wanted to see him. Apologies always seemed to come too late and he knew I wasn't really sorry. By the time he came to my flat I was on the brink of tears. You must be nicer, I said to myself, you mustn't fight. Stop being so angry with me, he said.

That summer, the summer after I had first seen him in a cool dark restaurant, he forgot about his rules of brevity. We walked through Soho together, our hands in our pockets, gazing at each other. We walked and walked, didn't sit leisurely in cafés or shoot the breeze idly, we walked together through the maze of streets and alleyways and stared at ourselves in windows, looking away, unable to speak. In Soho Square we strolled up to the central construction, the lopsided little Tudor house with black beams and windows and a circular verandah.

'Charles the second used to meet his mistress here,' he said and we smiled at each other.

He talked about his life, his life before children and women, his first week as an undergraduate at Cambridge. He was unhappy and unsettled. One morning, he woke to find the entire grounds covered with a thick carpet of snow, and like every person from the developing world who has never seen that scene, he leapt out of bed, wanting to touch it. A group of students were collecting outside the square where the esteemed Fellows lived in this, the most prestigious college of all, with the nicest, oldest square. During the early hours, after the snow had had time to settle and become thick and crisp, some bright spark had cycled through it, engraving CUNT in huge curly letters in the snow. Slowly, one by one, each of the Fellows lifted his curtain, observed the offending word below, and retired back into the hallowed darkness. Nobody came outside. They simply waited for the snow to melt the word away!

He liked to talk about Cambridge, the nicknames and anecdotes, the pomp and ceremony. Because they couldn't pronounce Kaushik, and because in their tongues it sounded like Cowshit, he was nicknamed Dunggers. It sent me into fits of laughter.

'Were you embarrassed sometimes?' I asked. 'Being a Wog, I mean?'

'I beg your pardon?' he bristled.

'A western oriented gentleman,' I snickered.

I had been to a university where differences of culture were revered and celebrated with a vengeance. Many of the black students had changed their names to African ones, and Indian students were given time off to celebrate their myriad festivals. In the toilets around campus, there was graffiti over toilet-roll holders that said 'Sociology degree: Please take one'.

'I was always very proud of the fact that I had been to Cambridge,' he said pompously.

I had never met anyone who had actually studied at Cambridge, yet the university had played a significant role in my growing up. Every time we had visitors from India, which was usually once a month, RaviKavi's planned itinerary for them always included Kambridge. Along with Trafaalgurr Square and Pikidlee Circus and *Oh Calcutta* and jacket potatoes (which for some reason the Visiting Gods were particularly partial to) at Spud-U-Like. We would load up the car with enough food and drink to last a week instead of a poxy day trip, and my dad would negotiate the motorway hunched over the steering wheel, driving at ten miles per hour, ignoring all the hooting cars flying past. Halfway, he would pull up on the hard shoulder and then to my intense embarrassment, trestle tables and thermos flasks and parathas wrapped in kitchen foil with bundles of pickles and chillies would be hauled out. We would stand around the car, eating alfresco, RaviKavi and their friends oblivious to outraged English people sneering at such low-rank smelly behaviour.

On one of our many visits, we met a professor at the university. My dad had been trying to find him for years. His own tutor had studied at Cambridge, before becoming my dad's mentor at the Allahabad university in India. My father had learnt everything about Hindi poetry from him, so when his wife came and stayed with us, they decided to see if the old Cambridge professor was still alive. I was dragging behind the entourage, my mum's and the wife's silk saris glistening in the sunshine. After being thrown from pillar to post, they finally managed to meet the old man. Yes, indeed he remembered the young student, there were not many

Indians at Cambridge in the thirties. My mother and the wife and my father stood about grinning at the old man's bemused expression. Then my father did something that the wife talked about for years, brought up at every opportunity in her drawing room in Delhi. She used the anecdote to illustrate the difference between Indians who had been swallowed up by the West and Indians who were Indian through and through.

'You are my guru's guru,' said my dad. 'In my country, we touch the feet of our guru as a mark of respect. I should like to touch your feet.' And with a flourish, my dad had lowered his fingertips to the professor's feet and then touched his own forehead.

The old man's eyes had filled with tears. 'This,' he said, with an open gesture, 'this is India.'

Amrit stared at me when I told him that story and how embarrassed I had been that Dad should be so deferential. In my university, students regularly slept with tutors in order to get better grades and boycotted lectures if they thought them boring. The notion of respecting a tutor, much less being in thrall to him, was anathema to my generation. I assumed the same must be true of the university where Amrit taught.

'I should like to meet your father one day,' he said quietly.

We turned away from each other's eyes, because we would both have been too ashamed to present ourselves before RaviKavi and their Lucknow sensibilities.

Amrit's memories of Cambridge fascinated me. Our experiences were diametrically opposed. When news of his scholarship spread around the neighbourhood, a Christian lady had come to his parents' house to instruct him on how to use the bathroom. She had explained about the toilet seat and toilet paper and flushing and the ways of being a proper gentleman. He had been warned that he was to be an ambassador of his country and must carry the dignity of Indians upon his shoulders.

'Were you Harry Koo-Maar?' I giggled.

'I was not,' he retorted.

I, meanwhile, had been the product of multi-cultural education, where mothers from council estates regularly complained to the school because their child knew more about Diwali than Christmas. And at home, India had continued as surely as it had in Delhi and Bombay: Hindi was spoken, food cooked, values drilled, connections given, histories recounted, gods entertained.

There was no opportunity to tell Amrit of all these memories that came flooding into my head whenever we were together. They seemed to me tawdry rags in the face of the intricate fabric of his past. When he talked about his memories of India, I was transfixed. He finally told me about the woman he had married a hundred years ago.

CHAPTER FOURTEEN

He told me about Maya.

It was like every trashy Indian film plot I had seen, but the fact that it was true made me shiver with glee. She was fifteen and he was seventeen. He had been devastatingly in love with her. I wanted to know everything about it, like an explorer, like a miner in the gold rush. I wanted my suspicions confirmed, wanted to know that once he had loved, to prove that he had the capacity for loving.

Once upon a time, in a city situated in the northern part of Delhi, lived a boy and a girl who fell in love. They had to meet secretly, because she was a respectable girl from a decent family. Her people didn't approve of him, thought he was a loafer because he read American comics and hung around cinema halls with his friends, wanted to be a writer one day. They were the old-fashioned type, who thought that if a man crossed the seas, he would fall into 'buri saubut' – bad ways: drink alcohol, eat meat and lie down with white women. When he got the scholarship to Cambridge, the lovers became nervous at separation. She hadn't allowed him to touch her in the secret places, the exotic valleys and plains which could only be uncovered after the sacrament of marriage, and he was a young man with desire coursing through his veins. In a frenzy, they stole away to a secret priest, and got married in the afternoon, with only two close friends as witnesses. The priest instructed them to burn mango wood in the fire and throw sacred herbs to cleanse the spirit. They exchanged garlands made from rosebuds and jasmine flowers. They circled the fire five times, she shyly holding the tail of his saffron dhoti. They repeated arcane promises. Then the priest pressed together his two index fingertips, declaring that now their two souls were united as one.

Afterwards, they brushed off the sindoor from her hair, gave the garlands away, put the bangles, the red sari, the sacred coconut in the safe hands of the witnesses. The girl couldn't bear to part with everything, so she kept hold of the saffron muslin dhoti that he had worn in the ceremony. It was as light as gossamer, easily folded like a handkerchief. In a cheap hotel on the other side of the city, populated with prostitutes and disease, they fell into each other's arms. They were safe, married, nobody could break that holy contract. They would travel across the seas together, man and wife, nobody could stop them. They believed impossible things.

Bearing her secret, she returned home in the early evening, sat down to dinner, a woman. The family retainer happened to go to her room to pick up the soiled clothes she always left scattered on the floor. He spotted a corner of the tell-tale saffron dhoti stuffed away underneath the chest of drawers, and raced full speed with his discovery. All hell broke loose. Everything happened at once. Izzat was at stake, honour and shame dangerously close. She was forbidden to speak; the witnesses were summoned, impelled to silence. Her family had the marriage annulled, and swiftly arranged a suitable match. She was powerless against the conventions of society. He left India under a cloud.

They kept in touch by secret letters; he couldn't bear to be apart from her. She was full of guilt because her husband was a good man; he fell into buri saubut. When he finished at the university, he went back to see her, in an attempt to weave a rope of sand. In a taxi, he urged her to run away and break free and be with him always. She wouldn't do it, she was angry. That was that. He came back to England. They went on with their lives.

The ending was horrible, unsatisfactory. Frank was right, I was a hopeless romantic. Amrit laughed, said it was all a very long time ago, people change, it was for the best, things get lost in translation.

'Why didn't you fight for her?' I asked. It was important that he had fought for love, as though this information would renew my faith in him.

'When things get that broken they can't be mended,' he said.

It only happens once, I was thinking. 'Was she beautiful?'

'Yes,' he said, 'but beauty, like everything else, fades.'

'Why are you so miserable about everything?' I demanded. 'Why don't you see the good of things?'

'That's the prerogative of youth.'

'So she was beautiful, what else?' I said, as if I could count off on my hand the qualities of the woman he had loved and analyze them later.

'She was like a film star. I never thought she would even talk to me. It was so difficult to talk to girls in those days. Families always around, honour, shame, repercussions. You know.'

'And white girls were family free, they did wild things,' I said scornfully.

He shrugged.

'Am I like her?' I said mischievously, remembering he had used the line about the film star to me.

He laughed. 'You're crazy like her.'

I wished I'd known him then, although I would have only been a schoolgirl. He had never talked that way of other women, the people he referred to disparagingly, the people who were the mothers of his children. He said he had been devastatingly in love with Maya.

'Then what happened?'

'She led the kind of bourgeois existence that she had always wanted. Her husband was an IAS officer. They lived in a big house, had a large family. I expect she did some charity work. And so on and so forth. She tried later to get herself back into my affections, be friends. I couldn't allow that. I lost touch with her.'

He laughed and I could see his teeth, misshapen, crowding upon each other, nicotine-stained. His eyes as flat as the road. I was shattered at his revelations of not allowing love back in. I had a feeling that he must be made of marbled granite, possessor of a supreme will, almost inhuman, almost god-like. Nobody I had ever known was capable of such a freezing of emotion. It seemed to me magnificent and awesome for a human being to be in such fantastic control of his thoughts. It led, I was sure, to a honing of character.

All my life, I had been surrounded by emotions, they were littered around my house like confetti. RaviKavi were major shareholders in the ooze business. My mother sobbed openly for days when the council came and chopped down the three cherry trees at the bottom of the garden, so that there would be a clear light. My father hollered with laughter as he sat up all night with a friend who was visiting from India. They bickered constantly over irrelevancies. The house I grew up in was rich with emotions, they were thick in the veneer of the furniture, seeping from the wallpaper, resounding against the TV. I had always suspected that outside was the world, another world, but I hadn't thought it would be so different. For instance, I never imagined that there were people outside who would hurt you. I looked at Amrit and wondered how I had managed to live such a sheltered life, how I had managed my education and independence without encountering harm. Suddenly, my charmed life seemed to me to be half-baked.

I told him how much I admired him. I wanted to be a writer one day, be well versed in the ways of literature, confident with my prejudices. Although he had so enigmatically taken my manuscript off the hatch and put it inside his bag, he didn't say anything. No encouragement. No response at all. It's enough, I thought, that I know him, that I know a writer; that was encouragement enough. I didn't consider my parents and their dilapidated friends to be writers, although they were, many of them, great writers. They had all been published in their country, read and borrowed and quoted by each other. In England they had a pall of shabbiness and ordinary concerns which I couldn't fit into my idea of the writer's life. I imagined that Amrit was a land by himself that I wanted to live in, make mine. I volunteered information about myself, told him how well I knew my life was going to turn out, how sure I was that I was going to make a mark on the world. He would laugh without showing his teeth and my bravado would collapse within me, all the things I had known since I was a child seemed to become ash in his gaze.

He said that I would only begin to write well once I felt myself broken in two, once I wasn't sure, once I was full of doubt. He said that one had to discover the kind of writer one wanted to be and the only way of doing that was to examine one's perceptions about the world, have a point of view. He said the confessional form of writing was abominable, those catalogues of emotions trite. Women's writing didn't interest him. It was whining and apologetic, second rate. Writing, he said, was about ways of seeing the world, not about feeling the world.

'How do you know things if you don't feel them?' I asked.

'What makes you think anyone is interested in your feelings?' he said.

'It's what I'm made of, it's all of me.'

'Then you must make yourself of sterner stuff, or else you will be like a pig wallowing in his own mire.'

I didn't understand then, that the act of writing was 'the grasp at passing shadows' between the two, between plot and character, and that we weren't really talking of writing. We were talking about ourselves, who we were and the possibilities of who we could be. At the time I thought he was being superior, excluding me from his literary imagination. It was always that way with us. Always that patch of no-man's-land where there were real and frightening spectres of jealousy, resentment, repulsion. To me the broken glass that we trod on together looked like diamonds.

The summer progressed. The sex became better between us. He learned to put on condoms with an expertise he had previously lacked. I'd tell him he hadn't done it right. He'd sulk and tell me to shut up.

'I suppose you'll have a baby with some young person with a trendy haircut,' he scowled.

'I might.'

We would stare at each other defiantly and he would ask why I was so nasty to him and I would say that it was no better than he deserved.

'To me,' he said, 'everything seems to come down to biology. Every relationship I have with a woman.'

'Babies, you mean? Maybe you should read up on contraception,' I said scathingly.

'Love, romance, sex, it's all the same, it all ends up the same. In the same place. It all turns into responsibility and obligation.'

'You make it sound as though you have these things done to you, that you are not responsible.'

'I am responsible. I am responsible for everything. I'm so tired of it.'

We'd never fight for long, we'd turn away from the facts of his life and love each other in the dark. Be nice, as he put it. We would touch each other's face and close our eyes like blind people.

'You mustn't think badly of me,' he said, 'I'm not worthy of so much contempt.'

They would bubble up to the surface, the sentences I wanted to speak. I love you, I know you, I can transform you, let me in, let me love you, I don't care about anything.

Yet, even as thoughts, I knew they were clichés. I knew he would find it loathsome to be loved like that, so frilly and sentimental. I wanted to be the kind of woman he could love, someone who only loved him a little.

I wondered if what we had between us was a scene, if that was how he referred to it to friends, if indeed he discussed us at all, if there was an 'us'. Did it mean something when a man said he loved you and told you all about the things that mattered in his life, even when none of the things were promises, only expressions of love? When I asked him to clarify his feelings, he would become irritated.

'Don't rake all that up again,' he said, as though I was for ever turning worms between us.

I would lie in wait for his phone calls like an animal waiting for signs of life. And they would come, haltingly, begrudgingly, at the oddest times of the day and night, often once I had given up all hope of ever hearing from him. It was only days or sometimes weeks which would pass without his voice in my ear or his hand upon my face, but they were an eternity, doomed, hopeless times. It had been eight months since he had pulled me into the pub full of Irish gods. The Hope and the Despair. Every meeting seemed like a continuing story, every parting a little death to me. For him, it seemed to be a natural course of events. He never made any plans and it confounded me. I couldn't stop asking him, 'When again?' He would say he'd call me, he'd see me when he could.

'How dare he?' I railed at Frank. 'How dare he treat me like this? It's not fair.' Nothing lasts long with him. Luke had warned me.

'You're going too fast,' said Frank. 'You have to control the speed.'

He spoke as though a relationship was like a ride in a motor car. The metaphor didn't interest me. 'You don't understand,' I said unhappily.

'Neither do you,' said Frank.

The more Amrit made vague appointments, the more unavailable he became, the more panic I began to feel. I knew we were coming to the end of it and I felt cheated because there had been no beginning, not one between us, only the endless beginnings in my imagination.

'I've been thinking...' he said one night on the ansaphone that I had especially left on in a bid to show my supreme indifference towards him, a desperate measure to prove that I would not always wait for him to call. 'I've been sitting here and thinking about this relationship which is conducted by telephone and snatched meetings. Where will it all end?'

I grabbed the phone, his presence as irresistible to me as oxygen, the pull in his voice as unbearable as pain. 'What are you talking about? Aren't I being nice?'

'Why are you putting up with so little?' he said. 'I'm never going to give you what you want.'

'Others have put up with it,' I said biting my lip.

'I know you're trying. I know. It's no good is it?'

'Am I not doing it right, Amrit?' My voice caught in my throat in fear of what he was going to say.

'You think I don't know the things you want. I know you would like for us to be together, writing, loving, laughing. We'd have fun you know. Such laughs. We'd live in a house and people would come and visit all the time. It would be terrible because we'd fight, but we'd always find some common ground. I can't do it, my dear. I just can't. I won't. It's nothing to do with the situations I'm embroiled in, I can get out of them. It's not that.'

'Then what?'

'It's too much,' he said. 'I can't. I want you to disappear. I want you to be banished. It's not that I don't feel anything. It's just the way it has to be.'

'But why? Let's try, Amrit. Couldn't we try? Couldn't we be loving friends?'

'Relationships always develop. They have to go some-where. Or else they wither. Let me go. You must go on with your life.'

As soon as he put the phone down, I phoned him right back in a rage and shouted crazy things at him, how much I hated him, how I could do without him, how I wanted him out of my life for ever.

'Fuck off, then,' he said. 'Leave me alone.'

In a burning frenzy, I collected up the three precious things he had ever given me: his novel, the letter from Paris and the Billie Holiday tape he had pretended to make for me. I stuffed them inside a jiffy bag, posted them immediately. He never replied.

After two weeks of silence, I relented and phoned him.

'Are you still angry?' he said.

'Don't know,' I mumbled.

He said I was right to have done it, it was better for me this way. 'I know you reconsider things, but you mustn't,' he said gently. 'You must be on your way.'

I didn't want him to talk me out of my feelings, I didn't want him to be so assured. He said he had hoped I would write him a letter with the things and was glad I hadn't. It would be best if we just remained fond friends. Things would iron out, he said. Better all round. One day, soon, we would go out for lunch and laugh about this. I knew I wouldn't. I knew I wouldn't ever laugh and I knew I wouldn't forget the way he spoke, as if it were nothing to him.

'Don't you know anything?' I said. 'Don't you know?'

Later that evening he called me back. I had drunk a whole bottle of wine by myself and smoked a hundred cigarettes, kicking myself for sending back those things. I knew I would never get them back. It was as though he had never existed in my life. I hadn't realized how precious those things had been, and had scorned them for being so little, so cheap, so ordinary. I was sitting with my feet over the coffee table, full of wine and anger and hopelessness, when the phone rang. It's over, it's over, it's over, I was thinking. He never knew me.

'I was in a meeting,' he said, 'I had to leave. My mind wasn't on it.'

'So what?' I said nastily before he could sense my excitement.

'I sat down at my desk and looked out of the window and felt as though I could see across all the rooftops and chimneys and right into your window. There was nothing else, no sky, no families, no obstacles to you. I could see you sitting with your feet on your coffee table, already forgetting about me.'

As though scalded, I removed my feet from their position and curled them under me.

'What are you up to now?' I asked him dully and he laughed as though I had made a joke. But I was already listening keenly, weighing up his words as I always would. Another woman would have slammed the phone down to the nonsense.

'I miss you,' he said, 'I miss you.'

'You're feeling bad, that's all. Feeling bad about finishing things.'

'No. It isn't that.'

My heart sank at his admission. He had not phoned to take back his words.

He said he missed me because we were two parts of the same thing, and crushed with humiliation I shouted back that I was nothing like him. He laughed and said, 'Don't you realize that we are almost the same person?'

'It's not true!' I screamed at him.

'Don't you know anything? Didn't it ever occur to you that's why we fight?'

'We fight because I love you and you don't give a damn about anybody.'

'I'm a refrigerator,' he said. 'I'm a piece of wood. I'm a dead person.'

It stunned me. A vague memory came spinning into my head, hurdling my heart. It's no good. He's dead you see?

'What's the matter with you?' I said urgently, 'Why are you saying these things? You're no such thing. You're alive and funny and difficult and you drive people round the twist because you never listen to a word they say.'

'You're not people,' he said and we laughed at each other. 'Will you forgive me? Will you let me come and sit by you? Just for a while. Then you can kick me out.'

He caught a taxi and brought me cigarettes and two bottles of wine. I opened my mouth and he put his hand over it.

'Don't say anything horrible. Don't say, "Is this all I'm worth?" Don't say, "Why can't you buy me something expensive?" Don't say anything if you're not going to say anything nice.' He sat down on the sofa and put his head in his hands.

'Don't be like that,' I said. 'Be nice.'

I took his hands away, laced my fingers through his and looked at his face, so hard, I wanted to remember it. And I thought, it must be terrible to be loved like this, have someone's gaze upon you like a spotlight, have someone forgive your worst actions. Yes, I thought, with a kind of satisfaction as I traced his still, quiet face, it must be terrible for him. We made love for the last time. I knew it, I couldn't look at him.

When the condom broke, I leapt out of bed.

'Don't look at me like that,' he said. 'It'll be alright.'

'Shut up,' I shouted. 'Get out of here.'

'It wasn't my fault.'

'Get out,' I said. 'Get away from me.'

'It'll be alright.'

I felt cold all over, cold and wet, in a strange panic. 'Don't you dare talk to me like that!' I shrieked. 'Don't you dare patronize me.'

'Don't talk to me like you hate me,' he said.

It wasn't an argument that could have continued. He had to pick up his kids from a class and bundle them in the car. Then he had to pick up their mother and go to the country for the weekend in a cottage they had rented from a friend. Which mother, which children, I didn't want to know. I wanted to be alone until the morning came and I could go to the clinic to get it fixed.

'I'll try and phone you,' he said as I sat stony faced and fully dressed.

'I'd prefer you didn't.' I didn't want him to feel sorry for me, didn't want him to panic and hate me and speculate about the kinds of troubles I may try to land him in.

'I will phone you,' he said, 'I will. Because I want to. To make sure you are alright.'

'Go away,' I said in a brittle voice.

CHAPTER FIFTEEN

'Are you alright?'

The sun was shining brightly into the front room and all the dust sparkled on the surfaces. I was lying on my back watching TV, blowing perfect smoke rings at the ceiling.

'I'm fine. Sorry I was horrible. I was, you know, frightened.'

'What happened? Are you sure?' he said urgently.

'For god's sake,' I said, irritated with his urgency. 'Don't worry. You're not going to be landed with another child.'

'I'm not worried,' he said stiffly. 'So everything's alright?'

'Look,' I said, shooting the smoke out of the corner of my mouth, 'I went down the clinic. They gave me the morning-after pill. I was well within the time frame. No problem. Forget it. What are you doing?'

'Nothing. It's boring. I have to do it,' he said. 'I'll call you.'

'No you won't,' I said. 'Nothing's changed.'

There was a short silence. I couldn't even hear him breathe.

'I was watching TV last night. Everyone had gone to bed

but I didn't want to sleep, so I drank a bottle of whiskey and stayed up watching TV. You kept travelling across my mind.'

I laughed. I was so flooded with relief, so proud of having extinguished my anxiety, so relaxed. I was bored with saying what do you mean, like a parrot, only for him to take things back, only for him to confuse me, so I laughed.

'It's funny, this relationship we have,' he said. 'Spending all one's time in such distress and longing.'

Again and again he would unload such words from his lorry of knowledge and then disappear from my life until I, defeated by memory, devastated by unfulfilment, sought him out. Again, I would demand clarification. For those rocks in my heart.

'How can you have a relationship with someone when you never see them, when you keep changing your mind?' I shouted at him in exasperation.

'Stop raking all that up again,' he shouted at me. 'If you don't like the way it is, get out.'

And I thought, what a monster he is, how waterproof he is, how devoid of honour. He was what in the old days, I supposed, people called a heel. I looked at myself in shop windows and wondered who I had become. There was no word from him for two weeks. He thinks he's safe, I thought, as I bit the sides of my thumbs in front of the TV. He thinks he's got away with it by the skin of his teeth. I felt bitter about his households. He had a commitment to them, and in my mind, commitment was the same as love. He might have had his own room, he might talk of them in bad words, but those women had a claim on his time. He must fight with them too, I thought miserably. I wondered if fights were an occupational hazard for philanderers.

He called and apologized for his absences, gave me lists of excuses. The children were on school holidays, one of the au pairs had fallen ill, he was deluged with work. You have no idea about the things I have to do, you're so young and so free. I had the feeling he was trying to ingratiate himself and I seized upon the illusion of power.

'At least he cares about his kids,' said Frank.

'Piss off.'

'Kids are important. They're the only people that matter. If I had kids, I'd lay down my life for them. I'd be squeezing their chubby chops all the time saying haven't you groooown, like my grandma does with me,' said Frank, giggling.

'Don't be so Jewish.'

'Can't you meet anybody your own age? In the workplace, no boys there for you?' said Frank in his hilarious mix of IndianJewish-didn't-sound-like-either accent.

'No. Listen, you were right. It's different now. I'm in the driving seat. He's feeling guilty. Guilty as hell.'

'Now who's being Jewish?' said Frank.

When I talked of him I could be clever and cavalier, but when I was with him, my soul was wretched. We began to meet for hesitant moments again, in restaurants or by the coffee table. The thought of making love was too painful, we seemed to be on a battlefield. I wondered why he kept it up, why he didn't turn away and run. He would look at me mournfully, as though he expected me to slap him or dissolve into tears. He was suffering, taking the blows and I was glad.

I asked him question after question, daring him to say stop, that's enough. I kept trying to find out things about his life, his relationships, so that somehow I could edge into his existence, make a place for myself there, stab him back. He never actively censured information. It astounded me. He never said, that's private, that's between me and her. He would tell me all I wanted to know. Was it because he felt guilty, because he felt lucky that it hadn't become an uncomfortable situation? I remembered the pills I had taken with water, my hands shaking. High progesterone or high oestrogen, I couldn't remember. Strong chemicals that would stop anxiety. What if they don't work, I'd thought wildly, what will become of me? And as I swallowed them, I knew they would work. Modern science it was. Upturning laws of physics had been a childhood fantasy. Mere humans couldn't really do that.

When he looked into my eyes, or reached for my hand across the tablecloth I looked away. I wouldn't allow any amends. I believed information to be my insurance, my right, for I was convinced that one day he would seduce a stranger in the night, reveal intimate details about me too. In my mind I could hear what he would say: 'She was like a trouser crease, sharp but completely mad, so gullible, so childish. She had delusions of grandeur, she thought she could be a writer, she thought she was the first woman who ever loved a man. I used to give her 'those ones,' lines from movies, just to see if she could tell the difference between lies and truth and tamasha, and she never could. She believed everything, actually it was terrifying, grotesque, to think that a person could be so naive. Once there was a terrible scare, I thought I was done for, but we managed it alright. Everything got fixed.'

My defence against this future humiliation was to arm myself with information about his life, stuff myself with as much as I could know, like a greedy pig. What sort of background was Clarissa from? How do you spend the day when you take the kids to the park? How do you explain things to them? Was Jonesy clingy like a dog because she had always been the affair? What sort of dinner parties do you have? When did you stop loving Maya? It exhausted me, I thought I would explode with the nourishment of it. There was an encyclopedia's worth of information to be gleaned before we could even sit and be with each other. And it was all so late, everything was ending. I felt as though I was cramming my heart just to watch it burst.

'Have you finished your interrogation?' he said with a sad expression on his face, knowing I needed to know.

The end was coming, I had seen it coming. Sometimes I wondered if it had come and I had not noticed it. But I knew it had begun somewhere at that weekend in the country, drinking his bottle of whiskey. The end had begun when the condom broke. Things had become different between us after that. More brittle. I would pump him for information about his life, to see how much I could stand. And all the time, the information would devastate me, every new piece of truth sent him hurtling away into the realms of another woman, a previous history. He saw the expression on my face, as though I had been made to watch a terrible road accident, and he picked out a poetry book from my shelf.

'Let me read something to you,' he said, changing the mood.

'Read this one,' I said eagerly, 'this one about the head of the one I love.'

'It's so soppy, like a pop song. This one.' He opened the book of poems but he didn't need to read the words. He recited them to me.

> 'And thereupon my heart is driven wild:
> She stands before me like a living child.'

He knew the lines to use with me. He knew he could soft-soap me with literary devices, turn the key of my mood. But I wasn't the person I had been brought up to be any more. I had become an illiterate.

'What would you have done?' I heard myself say, though I'd promised myself I wouldn't ask, would never ask, never refer to it. 'What would you have done if I'd become pregnant?'

He sighed. 'I would have tried to do the best I could for you.'

'Would you have done it for love?'

'No,' he said, shaking his head, 'no, not for love.'

'You've meant those words when you've had a lonely moment. You've said things, but you've never loved me.'

'No,' he said, looking at the carpet, avoiding my eyes. 'When you love someone, you do something about it. You should have known that. I couldn't have ever loved you. Not really.'

The words came at me like a javelin. That evening, there
was a sudden summer storm. The trees outside my window,
laden with their burden of leaves, whirled like banshees. I
thought about the needles of rain splattering against his
windscreen, as the cracks of fluorescent lightning broke into
my dark front room. I stared at my eerie hands, the veins
throbbing in the unnatural light. How fast time had fled, how
long it had gone on, this not loving.

For a month I didn't see Amrit. I phoned up all my
friends and went out every night. I even punched out the
number of the squat but killed it before it rang: I couldn't
bear to see Luke, I didn't want to humiliate him. One
evening I went out on a date with Connor from work. He
was Irish, knew all about unrequited love, had read
everything by Joyce. He took me on the back of his
motorbike along the Embankment and we walked along
Hungerford Bridge and looked out at the dark dirty famous
river and the landmarks of London on the horizon.

At dawn we drove along the silent streets to Smithfield
Meat Market for a fry-up breakfast in one of the early pubs
full of traders in blood splattered coats. I said I'd always
wanted to see Smithfields, but now I couldn't face seeing all
that dead flesh hanging from hooks. He told me about how
Joyce had yearned to meet Yeats, had finally met him when
the poet was an old bumbling man, writing about
spiritualism: 'I have met you too late,' declared Joyce. 'You
are too old.'

When I said I wasn't sure about when again, he said he
would keep asking me, if I didn't mind and I said I'd like that.

Frank took me dancing and we sat in cafés in black
clothes, drinking black coffees in Soho among tourists. I
pushed my palms down the sides of my body and felt the
firmness of my skin encased in Lycra. I was young, I thought
vigorously. I will live and love and feel sad over love affairs.
It was nothing. People didn't have to love you back. You
couldn't make them. I wished we had always stayed friends,
wished it could all have changed back. When the blackness

swooped over me I closed my eyes tight.

'I'm suffering, it hurts like anything,' I said to Frank. 'Will it be over soon?'

'Yes soon,' he said.

A month after Amrit's weekend in the country, I turned twenty-five and on the same day my novel was accepted for publication. Torquil, the agent that Frank had picked up in a bar, had got back on track. He had been zig-zagging the manuscript to every publisher in town. I had a collection of rejection slips stapled together in a drawer. I had sort of forgotten I had written a novel and I was dazed at the news. Torquil's urgent voice on the phone said, 'Did you hear me, did you hear what I said?' Mrs Menozzi, usually so reserved and disapproving of anybody under fifty years of age, planted a kiss on my cheek and clapped her hands above my head. The next day I repaid her generosity by pretending I had a dentist's appointment and landed up at the university. The secretary looked at me sideways. She knows, I thought.

'He's in a meeting.'

'I'll wait,' I said smugly.

Although I was bubbling with my news, I was rehearsing exactly how I would be in his office, calm, casual, indifferent. By the way, I would say, inserting the news cleverly between sentences.

'Hello,' he said poking his head out of the door, his eyes shining.

'You've got a meeting in five minutes,' piped the secretary.

'Screw the meeting,' he said, without taking his eyes off my face. He held the door open above my head and then closed it behind us.

I sat down carefully on the sofa and he resumed some paperwork on his desk, just as though I was another dreary person who had come to see him. Although I was used to this routine by now, it never ceased to irritate me, because I never understood the point of it. Do you think it's cool to ignore me once I am in your field of vision, I had asked him. I'm always trying to adjust myself in your presence, he had grinned, daring me to believe such a fantastic lie. But that day was different, because I was so excited. I was smiling as I watched his shoulders pushing his pen over paper. I glanced confidently around the room, taking in the postcards and memos on the wall and then suddenly I saw it.

On the shelf above his head lay my manuscript, untouched, unread, along with other pending matters. My lip quivered. That disastrous night we had made love for the first time when he had picked up the manuscript from the hatch so proprietorially and I had been so timid about how he would like it. We'd talked about writing and how ideas appeared out of your life and got twisted into fiction. He had said plot was everything, the what-happened-next aspect of story and I had said character was everything. I had waited with baited breath to see if he would mention the merits of my work. I had bitten my lip, in case he should think I was waiting. All these unrelated incidents knotted inside my throat as I stared at the manuscript, sitting on the shelf like wastepaper.

Finally he turned around to face me and I looked at the floor, my eyes bright. Don't cry, don't make a fool of yourself, it's nothing, don't react.

'Sorry to be so busy,' he said with a broad smile. 'It's so good to see you. I've thought of you so much. You've been angry, don't be. Let me make it up to you.'

Don't let him know you can see it, I told myself. Don't let him think it matters to you. Don't tell him why you're here. Make up a story.

'I've been accepted for publication,' I said crossly. The words had come out before I could stop them. I knew I should have said it politely, said it without giving myself away, but I didn't know how.

He lifted an eyebrow, flicking some papers at his desk. 'Who by?' he grinned. 'Don't tell me, The Black Women's Press.'

I looked at him. I knew exactly what he thought about such publishing houses. How they made concessions for untalented opportunists. I stared right into his eyes. The room began to waver under my gaze and I stood up unsteadily.

'Where are you going?' he said astonished.

'I think I'm going to be sick.'

CHAPTER SIXTEEN

After coming out of the toilet, I kept on walking. I wondered how long he would sit at his desk waiting for me to come back, but all I remember was watching my feet treading the pavement, one foot in front of the other, getting on to a train smelling of sweat and perfume. Bare shoulders jostled me and I gulped in chunks of the airless air. It was an extremely hot day, people's ugly faces on the tube were perspiring and pink like pigs and I ran over what I had eaten, what I had drunk, that I should be vomiting in an office toilet in mid-morning. I felt faint although I had never fainted in my life, not even when I had upturned the law of physics, me with my finger and the socket of the lamp. My skin seemed to be prickling, as though electricity was charging underneath the surface. As soon as I turned the corner to my road, I nearly died with happiness.

Tash was sitting cross-legged on the lawn, the rucksack next to her, serenely reading a book. Mark Tully's *No Full Stops in India*.

'Lots of commas and semi-colons,' I cried, and she leapt up to embrace me, held me for minutes and then tore herself away so that I could see what she looked like. Of course she had lost weight, of course she was tanned, of course she looked like she could sleep for a week.

'You look like shit,' she said. 'Can I stay?'

Even though it was Tash who had got off a plane after flying for eighteen hours, who had endured sitting in a smoking seat, feeling defiled because she had given up ciggies as well as meat in India, it was I who was packed off to bed with a jug of cool water by my bedside. As I drifted off to sleep, I was smiling at how our roles had reversed. After she had left school and started a life of travelling, every time she came back to London, Tash had to look for homes, places to put her stuff, lay her head. Her mother was always living with a difficult man and her sister was married with three kids who took up the whole house. So from the age of sixteen, Tash had learnt to adapt herself to people, be grateful for a room, for hospitality offered. She had stayed in my parents' house several times, even when I was at university. Snubbing her god-like status as Hindu guest, she cleaned up the house and put the books and magazines in order whenever she stayed there. My mother liked stuffing her full of food. Despite her broken home, her permissiveness and her tight cleavage, my mother had always maintained that Tash was the only one of my friends who had a good character.

When I woke up, the sunshine still streaming through the windows, I found her bathed and scrubbed, with a towel round her head in a turban, watching TV intently in the front room, her feet up on the coffee table. There was a cheese sandwich on a plate in front of her.

'It's always cheese sandwiches,' I said, cuddling up next to her on the sofa. 'It's always that.'

'The only other thing I missed was a good pint,' she said making her face like a muppet.

'You're sooo English,' I sneered. 'How was it?'

'It was so different, I never knew it would be like that. So many people. I didn't stay in the North much, I wanted to

get away from the urban sprawl. After Delhi, I went South. I
went all along the coast, from Madras to Mahabalipuram,
Madhurai, Kanya Kumari, Kovalum. It's the hippie trail,
there were loads of weirdos, but you don't have to be part of
that. I stayed in fishermen's huts on the beach. I spent
afternoons in temples, those huge massive living temples;
they really work, they aren't just edifices. The women in
Mysore, from the youngest to the oldest, all wearing orange
flowers in their hair, peanut sellers tick-tacking the air. I
didn't bother with the malaria tablets after a while, they
make you sick. It was totally liberating. I don't care if you
think it's a typical white person's view, but it was spiritually
uplifting. It was! I felt straightened out. I didn't freak out
once! I didn't get ill and I didn't lose my passport. I felt
humbled and awed. All sorts of strangers showed me such
kindness. I felt privileged. So weird being back. Everything's
so quiet, so creepy. Everyone's inside watching TV.'

As she regaled me with long rambling tales of her
adventures in India, I was breathing evenly, watching my
chest go up and down. I wanted to hear everything, take it
in, but my mind kept wandering. I knew she must be feeling
disorientated, needing a calm environment to lay her head,
to let the tumultuous images of India subside in the quietness
of London streets, and that she had expected this in my flat,
which she had created, knew well and felt cosy in. Yet my
heart was fluttering madly, restlessness sweeping me away.

'I couldn't stand Delhi. It was like Hong Kong upside
down! Your parents are fine. I spent a few days with them.
They insisted on taking me everywhere. Didn't like to tell
them that all I wanted to do was lie on the bed under the fan
all day and all night.'

'You know what they're like,' I said, rolling my eyes.
RaviKavi were like New Yorkers. It was their mission in life
to wear out any visitor who came to their door, by stuffing
them full of everything the city had to offer: scenic bus
routes, clever wheezes for getting into the theatre on a
discount, Sunday openings of museums (half price),

interesting walks, the Number 11 which took the exact route
of the London Sightseer for a fraction of the price, packed
lunches, maps, guide books, huge breakfasts of toast and
parathas and mutton chops.

'What's the house like?' I asked groggily.

'Still being built, but the flat's nice and roomy, through
breeze, guest bedroom. They've got it all done out nicely,
quite minimalist for them.'

We both giggled at my parents, the sultans of slob, being
referred to as minimalist. I felt my stomach burble.

'I feel sick, I think I'm actually going to be sick. Again.'

Tash rubbed my back as I knelt over the toilet bowl.

'You're not pregnant, are you?' she laughed.

'I can't be,' I said. 'I don't think it's possible.'

The doctor at the clinic said it was more common than was
realized. She gave me a photocopied article from the
Guardian women's page, as though it went some way
towards proving her point. I stared at the statistics and
looked up at her.

'How soon can I get it fixed?'

'Of course, you'll have to have another test, to make
certain. And then you'll see a counsellor, who will help you
weigh up your options, provide you with information about
child care and...'

'No,' I said, frowning at her as though she couldn't
understand English. 'Let's skip all that. I don't need a
counsellor. Save it. I know what my options are and I am
opting for a termination. I'd like to know the fastest route.
Please.'

The doctor looked at me over her glasses and blinked.
'The counsellor,' she continued frostily, 'will take you
through the procedure of whichever option you choose.
There is a reason we do this, you know, it's not for our
entertainment. Perhaps you haven't thought through everything. This isn't something you should take lightly. You
might have been careless in the past, but that is no reason to

go barging into something like a bull in a china shop.'

I sucked my bottom lip and looked at her and then at the clock behind her ticking away the minutes. How soon can I get out of here, I was thinking.

'Right. OK.'

'Right,' said the doctor, her face broadening into a satisfied smile.

Once we were out of the surgery, my arm linked in with Tash's, she asked me how it had gone.

'Old dragon,' I said. 'I think she was a pro-lifer. It's like arguing with fundamentalists, what's the point? Anyway, when she asked if I'd be opting for private or National Health, I stared right into her beady little eyes behind those doctor specs and said, "Private, of course." I made a big performance out of the word, then said, "You have to pay for professionalism these days."'

'You didn't!' laughed Tash. 'Serves her right. What shall we do now?'

I looked up at the gathering clouds in the late evening sky. I remembered that phone call he had made. I can see you, all across the rooftops and chimneys with your feet on the coffee table, already forgetting about me.

'I'm going to buy you a pint,' I said.

It took us under two hours to start giggling under pressure of alcohol. The pub had filled out and was full of sweaty flesh, men in shorts and the gunfire sounds of fruit machines, MTV and jukebox songs, shrill laughter.

'You'll have to tell him,' she said. 'When will you tell him?'

'I'm not going to tell him.'

She stared at me and drank her pint. 'You have a relationship with...'

'Haven't you listened to a word I've said? He has relationships with other women. He has no relationship with me. I was a brief encounter. It's none of his business. He wouldn't care about it.'

'I'm sure you're wrong about that.'

I stared at the people milling around us, the heat rising

from the floorboards like vapours in hell. Everyone seemed to be shouting, taking up all the space, and lights were flashing. Like evidence, his face kept threatening to loom up inside the filmy developing fluid in my head. It had that endless expression, like miles and miles of sand, no horizon and no perspective. I thought, no, I am not going to allow him in. Never. I squeezed my eyes shut as if to push the object back into the depths, plunge it back into darkness.

Tash took my hand and said, 'I'm sure you're wrong about that. I think he cares more for you than you think.'

I smiled at her. What a nice idea it was, an idea I could get lost in if I wasn't careful. There's always two sides of a story, there's always another way of looking at things. I remembered my father's face on that first trip home, back home to Lucknow, the huge ramshackle house of his childhood where lizards jerked along the corner of the terracotta walls, and dim oil lamps illuminated the central courtyard. I was ten years old, holding on to my mum's finger, hiding behind her sari. All the faces staring at him, looming up in the darkness, one set of eyes above another. What have you bought daada? What have you brought from Villayat? Here's a spoon to eat your khaana with, you must have forgotten how to use your hands. My father had lost his temper. He had railed at the bewildered assembled throng. 'Who do you think I am?' he had shrieked. 'What do you think I am made of, that I should be so easily seduced? Do you think four years in a foreign country has made me into an Englishman?' And then later, my mother soothing my dad's anger, in the dark cramped room, next to the muddy toilet which didn't have a door or a lock and where flies and insects hovered happily around excrement. A tear popped out of his eye and plopped down to the stone floor. 'There are always two sides of a story,' she said. 'England is so far away, it's only natural to think. You must adjust.' But my father was inconsolable. He felt betrayed by those he loved. He felt thwarted, exiled through misunderstanding.

'What's the matter with you?' I had demanded, my legs

swinging from the charpai, the rough weave of rope cutting into my thighs.

'Be quiet,' said my mum. 'Go and help in kitchens. Go and assist your aunt and grandmother.'

'No way!' I had screamed. 'I won't go. I don't like it here. I haven't been to the toilet for two days. I can't go in that hole in the ground!'

'Come here,' said my dad. 'Come and sit down near us.'

Clicking my tongue, I had walked across to their huddle on the other charpai, sinking with their weight. My dad had put an arm around me.

'These people, your uncles and aunties and neighbours who you don't know, all these people who keep asking you the same question...'

'Do you like it here or do you like it there?' I mimicked in Hindi, twisting my face in disdain.

'All that and this, the toilet without a door and the flies. Your feeling of disgust and discomfort and despair. Remember it. Remember all of it. Don't let anyone make you forget it.'

'Is that why you're crying?' I said, suddenly serious, knowing he was saying something of importance, but not being able to hear, because my dad was crying. It was unbearable, unthinkable.

'I'm not crying,' he said and smiled at me. 'Sometimes remembering makes you weep.'

'Sometimes you have to forget about people,' I said and Tash smiled. 'Forget about feelings and smells and fires.'

'Only you never really forget, do you?'

'It finds a place somewhere. Do you remember what you told me? About travelling. Going to dangerous places out of curiosity. I was in my curiosity season,' I said and laughed, then immediately asked, 'How's my mum? How's my dad? Are they alright?' The thin blue aerogrammes were piled up inside my bedside cabinet in a shoebox. My mother's shaky handwriting asking me if the blossom was out in their street, were the escalators working yet in Archway station, was

EastEnders still smashing? I had skim-read them impatiently, amused that she should be so concerned about a country that she had never had much time for. But of course it had been her country too, for many years, the country where she had worked and raised her child. The fortnightly phone calls had come regularly, short and swift and touching base. I couldn't even remember them as soon as they finished.

Tash screwed up her face. 'They're fine. They seem to be very busy. I remember them in London sitting watching TV all the time. In Delhi they're constantly on the move. Something's happening all the time. I think they'll settle down when the house is built.'

'My dad's making a film, so my mum says.'

Tash burst out laughing. 'He's got video upon video. He shoots all the time. I'm in it too, in one of the segments entitled "Mira's Friends From London". Imagine that, you've got a series dedicated to you, and you're not even in them. The absent presence. My dad never even noticed I was around when he lived with us. He never thought I would ever achieve anything in my life.'

'Was that why you went travelling? Is that why you never put down roots?'

'I think so,' she said. 'I wasn't as lucky as you. I didn't have something to refer to.'

'How's your mum?'

'The woman is living on remission. They're planning to buy a house in a village in southern Spain. I give it three months. My mother won't be able to cope without the gym!'

We laughed out loud. At school, Tash's mum was the most glamorous parent who came to the gruelling PTA meetings. She couldn't stand to be ferried along with all the other parents, preferred to make her own late entrances that used to mortify Tash and elate everyone else.

'I don't think I'm much of a traveller. Some people are no good at that sort of thing. I never found a place better than home,' I said. 'But I keep looking, because that's the fashion.'

'You have to find material, to write about,' she laughed.

'Shit,' I said suddenly. 'Guess what? I completely forgot. The novel's going to be published. That novel is actually going to be on a bookshelf. Can you believe that?'

Tash looked up from her pint, a smile slowly taking up her whole face. 'Do you think anyone you know ever doubted it?'

CHAPTER SEVENTEEN

Like a tomb which had been sealed from the world and now excavated, my life suddenly took on a new urgency. Tash threw open the windows and hoovered up the flat. She put up the Rajasthani wall hangings and tiny squares embroidered with shells and mirrors that she had haggled for on Delhi street markets. She said it was time I had some ethnic stuff in the flat, so that when strangers came they would know I was a Pukka Indian Writer. I felt like a pretender on all three counts.

Every other day there were phone calls from the agent, the publisher, the PR person, and like a clown in the circus I let myself be carried away by the tumult. Every time I put the phone down, I screamed at Tash and she screamed back, as though we were both thrust into some helter-skelter adult world, where adults were asking my opinion on book jackets and illustrators, requesting biographies, suggesting publicity strategies. It hadn't occurred to me that there would be this hive of activity before the book was placed on a shelf among other writers, even those ten-pence books on reduced stands on the pavements of the Charing Cross Road.

'My publisher, darling,' I announced with mock pompousness, putting my hand over the phone.

'Darling,' batted back Tash, her nose in the air, as if we were residents of a new gilded world, where neither of us had a plan or a clue. The only behaviour we knew was parody. I told her she couldn't move out just yet, I wanted her near. Not to talk over things. I just needed to know she was on the sofabed when I lay awake at night.

'Going somewhere nice, ladies?' said the beautician, chiselling away at our corns, while we admired our finished hands, stretching them out in the air.

'My friend's just got a publishing deal,' said Tash automatically. It was her stock answer these days to everybody we met, regardless of the question.

'Oh. That's nice. There's nothing to beat a nice manicure, though, is there?'

We laughed and said no, that was true, nothing to beat a nice manicure.

In between handsome lunches with my publisher, back-slapping coffees with my agent (I had become quite proprietorial) and feverish adjustments on the computer to bad grammar and punctuation, I went to have another test which came up positive. I withdrew money from the deposit account that was supposed to be for emergencies, and went and sat with Tash in a crowded room full of muted anxiety and people smoking outside the door, amongst other women who had begun the journey towards a private operation. No one spoke. There were all kinds of women there, all of us looking and looking away. Teenagers with their parents, women with men, women alone, women with friends.

'It's like the bleeding dentist,' whispered Tash as we sat by the door, watching the clock tick over on the wall.

'Look at these.' I offered her the collection of women's magazines I had picked off the central low table. They were all out of date, dog-eared, full of lurid Real Life dilemmas. My fight to have a baby. Life with quadruplets – a mother's story. I tried to kill my daughter because she was a heroin addict.

'You'd think they'd sort through them,' I said crossly.

Tash tore the wodge out of my hand and placed them back in a pile on the table where they remained untouched. Nobody was reading the magazines. They reminded me of my manuscript on the shelf above Amrit's head.

During two visits, I saw two counsellors, another doctor and finally got the forms for the clinic in Richmond. Tash linked her arm through mine as we walked out of the Pregnancy Advice Bureau.

'Shouldn't you tell him?' she said, looking straight ahead.

'Why, do you think he'll try and change my mind?' I laughed.

'Do you want him to?'

'Of course not.'

It wasn't the exact truth. I jumped every time the phone rang, relieved and disappointed, making silly jokes every time it was something to do with the book's publication. You should be enjoying this, savouring every minute, it'll never happen again, I told myself; this is what you've been waiting for. I remembered the sharp pain in my back all those months ago, as I had marvelled at my body, exhausted after sitting hunched over the computer; remembered it now in a sepia haze, the sweet pain of effort. And now the book was going to be born, sit in its newly-printed skin, fat upon bookshelves. But I couldn't feel it. All I was aware of was that imminent birth and imminent death were poised opposite each other, holding their breath, chancing their moves.

Apart from her support and kindness and closeness, the main reason I wanted Tash with me was so that she could be a witness to my success, so that in years to come she would remember it better than I. In the future, she would bring it up, make anecdotes of it and I would remember how excited and happy I had been.

The night before my appointment in Richmond, Tash told me to shut up and watch TV while she made us a slap-up meal. It was to be dahl and rice and cucumber raita, papads and fried okra. She had written down the recipe for the dahl when she was in India, and she knew that okra was my favourite, ladies fingers as they called it over there. She didn't want any criticism of her cooking, she'd warned. I turned off the TV and wrote a letter to my parents.

August 14
London

Dear Mummy, Papa,

Sorry I haven't written for a while, but now I have something good to tell you on Independence Day. The novel has finally been accepted for publication. The agent rang me at work on my birthday, would you believe it. Tash's here at the moment, so she is sharing in all the good news. Everything has become frenetic and I have become very busy talking to my publishers and deciding on the illustration for the cover. They have found me a lovely artist who has sent me some samples of her work. I had to write a biography about myself, which was difficult because I didn't really know what to say, so I went through the books on my bookshelf to see what other writers write. The ones who don't tell you much are boring, I like the ones who tell you interesting things about themselves. But I wasn't sure what to say about myself that's so interesting, so I just wrote a boring one instead about where I was born and where I live.

Anyway, all is much excitement here and the book should be out within six months they say. I get some free copies, but not that many, so don't promise everybody a copy, will you? Tash says the flat is very nice and that the house is nearly built. I'm looking into cheap tickets and maybe I will come when the prices drop, after January. Everything is going really well, there are no problems and I am very happy. There have been no expenses on the flat, although I think it needs to get painted in nicer colours. I might use the advance they are going to give me for that purpose – don't know exactly how much it is going to be,

I've left it in the hands of the agent.

Send all my best wishes to everybody and look after yourselves. Papa seems to have outdone Satyjit Ray himself, from what you say. Does everybody have to sit through the family archive every time they come to the flat? I hope you can move into the house soon. Don't worry about me, I am very happy and contented with life at the moment.

Lots of love.

We sat down to Tash's meal of under-cooked rice and oily okra, but superbly flavoured dahl, crispy papads and cooling raita. We ate at the coffee table spread with newspaper, using forks and spoons. Neither of us wanted to spoil our nails with turmeric stains. Then we drank two bottles of wine. We didn't discuss tomorrow. It was all in place, the plan. Tash had borrowed a car from a friend for the day.

The phone rang while we were finishing off and my heart thudded against my ribs. I lifted my eyes at her. It's him, I thought wildly. It's him at the eleventh hour. And I knew I didn't want to be talked out of it, knew I wasn't going to tell him any of it. But I also knew suddenly, appalled at myself, that all that mattered to me was to hear his voice. Just one last time, before I went to Richmond.

'Halooo, halooo,' cried out my mum's voice on the ansaphone and I ran and snapped up the phone.

'Yes, yes, I'm here,' I shouted, despite myself. When we used to live together I would tell my parents off for shouting down the phone to India. Didn't they know anything, didn't they know long distance calls were nothing out of the ordinary? My mum used to say that part of talking on the phone in India was the shouting, because the lines were always bad in India. But you're not living in India now, I'd say, you don't have to shout now.

'Monitring, she's monitring,' announced my mum, obviously to my dad who must have had his nose next to the phone.

My dad had never got the hang of the telephone, not even after ten years in Bombay and twenty years in London. He still didn't understand that the instrument could be used for purposeless chatter. For him, the phone was a means for making arrangements and although he was happy to listen to others blathering on, he would never himself make a long phone call. He used to say that it was a funny way to spend the time. Simply not done to waste money like that. And whenever they spoke long distance to my uncles and aunts in India, after the how-are-you-is-everything-alright-is-there-anything-you-need conversation, he would slink crossly out of the room while my mum chattered away about rubbish, wasting time and money. In this regard mum and dad had opposing views. It was probably one of the very few things they disagreed upon.

'I've just written you a letter,' I laughed, 'and now you've phoned.'

'What, what?' laughed my mum. 'This delay is very irritating. What have you written? Give me the highlights.'

'My book's been accepted,' I said, lowering my voice now, rolling my eyes at Tash.

'Don't be funny,' shouted my mum. 'Are you telling me that agent of yours has finally earned his money?' RaviKavi who, along with their writer friends, had all published their own books, never heard of agents in India. I had explained patiently that that's how they do things here. RaviKavi had a hard time understanding that books, like soap powders and machine tools, were just another commodity. They believed that writing was a noble art, getting published a formality, publicity an anathema. They were still living in the Dark Ages.

'And you were writing to tell me! Don't be funny.' She raised her voice, turning away from the receiver, 'Arrey, listen, listen to this. The novel. At last. Come, come.' Then back into the receiver, 'What do you think, we are living in Timbuctoo, or what? It didn't occur to you to call us immediately?'

'Haloo, what, what is this?' said my dad's excited voice. 'Write everything down, all the nitty gritty. Send us a letter, right away.'

'She has written it,' said my mum impatiently. 'My point is where is the telephone call? She was going to make me wait for ten days about the good news. What is wrong with you? You have become your father's daughter, afraid of the telephone.'

'Quite right,' said my dad, and we all burst out laughing. 'Everything else OK there? Need any money?'

'Everything's fine. Anything to report?'

'Nothing as exciting as yours. I'll write you a letter soon,' said my dad.

'Now, have you started the next one?' said my mum, and I screamed down the phone.

'Mum!'

'Of course, of course,' she giggled. 'But a writer must always be writing.'

Then the phone started fizzing and another voice came on the line, speaking in Hindi, wanting to speak to somebody called Mr Ahuja. My mum switched to Hindi, asking the caller to please get off the line as she was engaged in an important call to London, England, but the woman refused, saying she had to speak to Mr Ahuja, as though Mr Ahuja was hiding out in my mother's flat. Then my mum raised her voice, speaking over the woman.

'Crossed line, crossed line, can you hear?'

''Bye, Mum,' I said, 'I'll phone you soon.'

Tash and I cleared up the newspaper and dumped the dishes in the sink.

'You alright?' she said, pouring out the last of the wine.

My heart was beating fast. Nearly there, nearly at the end. Hold on. Hold on.

'What would you do, if it was you, Tash?' I said suddenly.

She shrugged. 'Have it, I suppose.'

'Have it? How could you? If you were me and he was him, you couldn't! **What** about all his other children, it's disgusting. Isn't it? And he wouldn't help you because of love, he'd only give you money because he thought he should.' I was rambling, trying to stop.

'Your idea of a family is not the same as mine. I grew up with a single parent. My dad's been married three times. I have several step-sisters and step-brothers. It's not that unusual.' She looked at me patiently.

I looked at the floor, burning with shame because I sounded so old-fashioned, so rigid in my views. 'It wouldn't be a family, would it?' I said stubbornly. I would be another conquest, I was thinking, just another one of his women, his breeders. The thought filled me with such a surging of hatred towards him I thought I would faint from the rush.

'There are lots of different types of families,' she said. 'What you mean is that it wouldn't be true love.'

We smiled at each other. I rolled my eyes. True love, it sounded so stupid, melodramatic, something I should have got over after my teenage years. It wasn't true love between us, it was something else, something I had never been able to pin down. I wondered with a jolt if it would ever seep out of me, the way the matter inside my ovaries was to be resolved tomorrow in Richmond.

'How do they put up with it, those women? Do you think they must really love him to put up with the indignity of it?' I said, humiliation stabbing at me all over. All these situations and scenes he had been through, all these intimacies he had shared with these faceless women he called people. I hated him. So clear and strong was the emotion that I was bewildered by it. Yet the hate filled me with strength, modulating my heart.

'No,' she said, 'I don't think everyone lives in teepees and wigwams.'

'What?'

'In tents. You're intense. Not everybody is.'

'But, still...'

'I think it's like he said. There was a situation, it changed, they're all living with the consequences. I think they probably don't mind it. After all, he pays for the kids' violin lessons and all that crap, holidays and stuff. And they don't even have to sleep with him. They don't even have to see him more than probably twice a week. Sounds perfect to me,' she giggled.

'I'd mind. I'd go out of my mind,' I said evenly.

'Yes, you would. You're not cut out for that sort of life. You haven't been trained for it. You've had the perfect family, doting parents. It's beyond your field of vision.'

'Ugh, you make me sound like a freak.'

'You are a freak,' she smiled.

'He wasn't trained for it. He came from a decent upright family, he...'

'Maybe he isn't what you think. Maybe he's not the fictional person you've made him out to be,' said Tash, looking at me. 'Maybe he's just someone who made mistakes in his life.'

'You gave me the wrong advice. You said I should have a look. That was the mistake I made.'

'You can correct mistakes,' she said. 'You can learn from relationships. At least you learn from them once they're over.'

I couldn't bring myself to look at her, because I knew my eyes would give me away. Did she think, did she seriously think it was over? Is that how it was with relationships, that you had them and they ended, like films and fast car rides? Of course I knew that, I had witnessed that in my own life. Luke and I had separated, glided out of each other's lives. One day we would be close again, remind each other of the happy times, give each other advice on relationships. But it wasn't the same with Amrit. It was another country, this loving. I couldn't imagine a time in my life when I wouldn't be loving him and loving him. I shuddered. Perhaps it didn't have to be that way, I thought, filled with hope. Perhaps I would get over it like other relationships. I liked that thought very much and hugged it close to me as I drifted off to sleep.

CHAPTER EIGHTEEN

The alarm went off at 6.30 a.m. and I sat bolt upright, my head completely clear. I went into the kitchen and started the coffee, thinking the noise of the grinder would wake up Tash in the front room, but when she didn't appear bleary-eyed in the doorway, I went to investigate. I knocked but no sounds came, so I pushed open the door. She was lying across the opened-out sofabed on her stomach, her T-shirt wringing wet and stuck to her body, the duvet on the floor.

'What's wrong?' I rushed to her side, placing my hand on her forehead. It was burning. I picked up the duvet and automatically covered her up. Her head still stuck on the pillow, she opened her eyes. They were bloodshot and streaming and her hair had gone into wet tendrils.

'I feel like I'm dying,' she groaned.

'You've got a very high temperature,' I said, feeling her forehead with the back of my hand. I checked her pulse, it was racing. I tucked in the duvet all around her, ignoring her protests.

'I'm sorry, I'm sorry,' she was wailing.

'You will be if you move a muscle. Don't worry, I'm going

to phone the doctor right now. I think you need to be in hospital.'

'I've got to drive you to Richmond.'

'Shut it,' I said, punching out the number on the phone with one hand, stroking her clammy head with the other.

When the ansaphone kicked in, I looked at the clock, clicked my tongue and punched out Frank's number on the memory. When his ansaphone came on, I tapped the phone impatiently until the beep came.

'Frank,' I shouted. 'Wake up, this is an emergency. Pick up the phone, pick it up now.'

'What the fuck...' his groggy voice came on the line.

'You've got to get over here right now. My friend's sick and you've got to help.'

'Do you know what time it is? It's the middle of the night.'

'I can't help that. My friend is running a high temperature and I have to be somewhere this morning. I need your help.'

'Listen,' he said dully, 'you don't phone me for months and then you ring me up in the middle of the night making outrageous demands. I'm not getting out of bed for another one of your dramas.'

I slammed the phone down and stared at it for a moment, my mind racing.

'I'll just have a coffee and get dressed,' said Tash, her voice frail and desperate. 'I'll get you there, I promised I would.'

I stroked her head and put a glass of water to her lips. 'You're going to be fine, I'll take you to Casualty myself. Damn, I knew there was a reason I should have re-taken that fucking driving test. Just stay there while I make us both a coffee. Don't move. Everything's going to be fine.'

In twenty minutes, I had showered, changed, got Tash into a thick jumper, put some stuff into one overnight bag for her and one for me, and rung for the cab. She looked like a rag doll, propped up on the sofa, swaddled inside all the clothes I had wrapped her in. It had begun to rain fiercely and the light outside was gloomy, filling up the front room with a grey deathly pallor.

'I'm so sorry,' she was saying. 'You've got to do it by yourself. I'm so sorry.'

'What's the matter with you?' I said in genuine wonderment. 'Don't you ever stop putting other people first?'

When we got to the Whittington, we went straight to Casualty, which was thankfully near empty. Trust Tash to be so accommodating as to fall ill at the least busy time. The receptionist balked at my tone. I could hear myself barking out instructions like one of those indomitable English ladies who ran fêtes.

'I am going to have to leave you in charge of my friend. This is her name and temporary address. There will not be anyone there till tomorrow. I want to be sure that she is given complete attention. She has just come back from India. Her particulars are...' I wrote down all the jabs I could remember that Tash had boasted about. At the back of my mind, I knew it could be malaria. Those tablets which had made her sick. The receptionist was kind, she took full charge and once I'd seen Tash taken into the care of a doctor, I left the hospital. It was raining in sheets now and I stood at the double doors looking at my watch. Bloody English weather. Bloody August for chrissakes! I was early for Richmond and thought I'd get the train.

In the hurtling carriage, staring at the dribbling window, I felt myself shrink inside the seat. All the anonymous faces were looking away from me, into their newspapers. I felt ugly and afraid. I hadn't planned any of this. I had imagined it vaguely as a day trip, with Tash at the wheel and soul music on the tape. I hadn't thought any further about it. And now Tash was laid up with malaria or typhoid or god knew what, just because she had taken my lousy advice over what jabs to take and not take, and I was heading towards Richmond by myself.

I can't do it, I thought suddenly, my body frozen numb. I pushed myself deep into the prickly seat. I'm frightened, oh god, I'm frightened. Nobody's here. Where is everybody?

Frank and Tash and Luke and RaviKavi, nobody was here. I was alone. How will I get through? I can't do it. But the train raced on, repeating its mechanical mantra. Gottadoit, gottadoit, gottadoit.

The clinic was a huge house, like a large womb with roman blinds in the window and pink walls in the hallway. The front room was given over to a reception area. Nobody wore nurses' uniforms and there was no smell of disinfectant, just two vases of flowers on the desk and kindly smiling women who came to receive me. I like it here, I thought madly. When they saw that I had arrived bedraggled, with my umbrella blown inside out, they seemed to bend over backwards to make me feel comfortable. I didn't like to say I felt better already, felt I could curl up in a corner and have a good old sleep. A woman put her arm around me and took me down the hall into a small bright room with four beds. Apart from the number of beds, it looked like a large bedroom. There was a television set mounted on the wall and ruched silk curtains around the bay window, with thick lace curtains in front of them instead of nets, so sunlight could stream in without anyone inside being observed. In any case, outside was a large garden away from traffic and prying eyes. Two of the beds were occupied and the women looked up as I was brought in. The one next to my bed was a young glamorous-looking redhead wearing a peach satin gown and nightie, reading a *Cosmopolitan*. The other woman was older and dressed in a woollen dressing gown, watching the TV, the remote in her hands. Both of them smiled and went back to their respective distractions.

'Now then,' said the woman who had brought me in, 'just get changed in the toilet over there and get into bed. I can bring you some magazines if you like. I'm sorry but you can't have anything to drink yet. You'll be taking the pre-medication soon. Just get as comfortable as you can. Buzz me if you need anything. We're here to help.'

With this, the woman flashed me a smile and walked out

of the room. I looked around and couldn't help grinning. Then I sucked in my lips, immediately guilty at smiling in such a place. I was thinking of poor old Tash on a stretcher left in the corridor of that draughty old hospital.

'Nice here, innit?' said the peach ensemble.

'Take a look at the menu,' said the woollen dressing gown.

Both of them looked at me surreptitiously. I reached over to the menu card on the bedside table. It was unbelievable. There was a choice of starters, main courses and desserts. And breakfast! I'd never in my life been in a hotel this good. I sucked in my lips again, trying not to smile and when I looked up both of the women had gone back to their activities. I understood that while occasional comments were OK, we were not here to make friends.

I shuffled into the roomy toilet and got changed into my nightie, half annoyed that I had not brought something nicer with me, and immediately scandalized at my blasphemous thoughts. When I came out, the woollen dressing gown had disappeared and I scrunched my hands into white knuckled fists until she emerged from another door, nodding at me, her vanity case in her hand. Two toilets in one room. It was outrageously decadent. I settled myself on the feathery pillows, the sheets crisp and fresh around me. I couldn't see the television very well, so I stared at the sheets instead, trying not to make eye contact.

'Here,' said the peach ensemble, handing me the *Cosmopolitan*, 'I'm pretty tired now.'

'Thanks,' I said, and before I could strike up a conversation, she eased herself down in the bed and closed her eyes.

Turning the pages of the glossy magazine, I wondered if each of us were taken to the operating theatre one by one or together. My wordless questions were answered half an hour later when two nurses came and wheeled the peach ensemble out of the room.

My thoughts seemed to be flipping like cards. How often and how casually that word had been used at school: Look at the state of him, he's a right abortion and a half. This is not a piece of acceptable work, young lady, it is an abortion. A horrible joke the boys used to make at school came rushing into my mind, something about a bowl of peaches being mistaken for a bowl of aborted foetuses. I went rigid with terror at the image, brushed the memory out by thinking of the range of lush trees outside my flat, nodding their heads peacefully, their leaves shimmering.

Then suddenly it occurred to me that there was always a chance that you didn't recover from a general anaesthetic. Cold panic shot up my spine. Only Tash knew I was here, so they would have to wait for a few days before they managed to locate her, or she located me. I'd be cold by then, probably decomposing. And then she'd have to contact my parents and they'd have to get a flight over, if they survived the shock of it, that is. What if they went to see Amrit to ask him to explain how I had got into this trouble in the first place. I felt queasy at the thought of my burial and the bewildered, tragic faces of my parents and Amrit's stony-faced demeanour. Stop raking all that up again, he would say, enunciating every word.

'Hello there,' said another woman and looked at my notes hanging at the side of my bed. 'Would you like to take this? You'll feel yourself dropping off quite quickly. Don't worry about a thing.'

'Are you sure I won't be awake? What if the general anaesthetic doesn't work?' I whispered anxiously.

'It'll work, don't worry. When you wake up, you'll be back here. You'll feel a little discomfort, because you'll be wearing sanitary pads. But afterwards you can sleep it off and then you'll have a lovely dinner in the evening. Alright?'

'Right,' I said and knocked back the pills she offered me. How on earth could it be that simple? I convinced myself that I would fly awake during the operation. I concentrated on what I would do to let the surgeon know I could feel everything. Would it be like a coma, would it be like those operations on television where the patient can see everything but not feel? That would be alright, because I wouldn't

have to look. I could poke the surgeon in the stomach if I
wasn't able to move any limbs. Or I could produce a noise
from my throat like a foghorn, the way I used to do when I
was little and absolutely bored, bored, bored...

When I next opened my eyes I wondered why the pills
hadn't worked and when the nurse would come along to give
me some more. Then I noticed that the ruched blinds were
closed and the central light was on. My eyes darted around
the room. The peach ensemble was sitting up reading *Cosmo*
and the woollen dressing gown was still asleep. I put my
hand between my legs and my fingers touched upon a
sanitary towel. I snatched back my hand and buzzed for the
nurse. Whatever had gone wrong, I needed to know about it
immediately.

'How are you feeling?' said the woman who had given me
the pills.

'What's gone wrong?' I asked her urgently.

'Nothing,' she said and smiled. 'You're absolutely fine.
Everything went smoothly. Now just relax. You will need to
change the sanitary towel, I've brought some for you. You
might feel a bit groggy, but that'll pass. If you feel bad, let me
know; sometimes people get a slight temperature, it's
nothing to worry about.'

'You mean it's over?' I asked in disbelief. 'I've been in and
out. It's happened?'

'That's right,' said the woman and went out of the room.

Relief and wonderment spread though me like liquid. It
was a miracle. I had survived. I tried to think of the hours
that had slipped between taking the pre-medication and now
and I couldn't think of them. It was amazing. I felt absolutely
the same. I didn't feel different at all. Intact. Still myself
completely. I slept for a while. It was a wonderful thick sleep,
full of warmth and cosiness. When I woke up I went into the
toilet to change my towel and I couldn't resist looking at the
blood. It was exactly the same as a normal period, only I
hadn't used Dr Whites for years. When I came back I

noticed that the woollen dressing gown wasn't there. I felt I was her custodian. I climbed back into my warm bed and watched the other toilet door anxiously. After a while when she didn't emerge I looked over quizzically at the peach ensemble who was now sitting up in bed brushing her hair.

'She's gone,' she volunteered. 'She was only in for the day.'

Wow, I thought admiringly, Afternoon Abortion. I wondered if she had had to go home to get the tea for her husband.

In the morning the first person I saw was Frank standing in the doorway. He had been waiting for me to wake up. He strode across to my bed, sat down unsmilingly on the chair.

'Don't you ever,' he said under his breath, 'slam down the phone on me when it's important. I'm not one of your stupid boyfriends.'

I opened my mouth to protest but then I just smiled at him, at his concerned face. 'What's a nice boy like you doing in a place like this?' I asked jauntily.

'Your friend phoned me. She's got some virus thing. She's back at your flat. Are you ready?' he said flatly.

'Haven't had breakfast yet,' I blurted out.

He stared at me as if I'd gone mad. The woman arrived with the tray of croissants and coffee I had ordered the night before. Frank sat stony-faced as I packed the food into my mouth. It took me a while to figure out that he was deeply uncomfortable watching me stuff my face in a place where they hoovered out the insides of women's bellies.

'I'll see you in the car. I just want to ... I'll just be a minute,' I said, slowing my steps in the reception area.

Frank nodded and smiled, gently took my bag from my hand and went out of the door. I could feel myself shaking and I held the corner of the desk with the vases of flowers.

'Yes, dear?' said one of the women who had administered to me.

'I was ... It's nothing. Doesn't matter,' I said shaking my head and turning away.

'It's alright,' she said, 'your friend will wait for you. Is there anything you'd like to know? Can I help you?'

'I just wondered if everything's...Nothing's...Down there, I mean.'

The woman patted my hand. 'Nothing's broken down there. Don't worry. You're alright. Take some rest. And go on. Go on with your life.'

'Thank you,' I said and walked out of the clinic.

'Are you alright?' Frank said in the car, solemn as though he was at a funeral.

'I'm fine. Thanks for coming.' I was thinking, Why am I fine? Why do I feel relief? What comes after fear?

'I didn't know all this. Why don't you talk to me these days?' he said, his bottom lip quivering.

I started laughing. 'Don't be so tragic. It's sorted.'

We drove the rest of the way in a silence that I didn't understand, a silence that I ignored. When he deposited me at my flat, he wouldn't come in.

'Go on,' I urged.

'I've got to be at work,' he said, looking away from me. 'You've probably got things to talk about with your mate.'

I stared at him uncomprehendingly. 'What things?'

'Girlie things,' he said and drove off.

Tash gave me a huge hug as I came through the door.

'What's the matter with him?' I jerked my thumb in Frank's absent direction.

'He's your friend,' she said. 'Are you OK, are you really OK?'

We ordered in pizza and sat in front of the TV with our feet on the coffee table. She told me about the draughty corridors of the Whittington, about the doctor who left her with a thermometer in her mouth for an hour while he was called away, the collection of doctors who gave her snide clinical looks when they realized that it wasn't typhoid, or malaria, or some flesh-eating disease.

'They're under-staffed,' we both said together and laughed at our collective guilt. Us girls who were the products of comprehensive school education where none of the teachers had ever complained about their salaries or the nightmare of the kids, but instead drilled into us in the Social Skills class that the Welfare State and the National Health were the jewels in the crown of Britain. It had been no better at home, where my parents were constantly swooning over the freedom that the dole and free medical health offered people. England is a wonderful country, my dad used to say to the Visiting Gods, for amenities. Not for culture or spiritualism or family loyalty mind you; England was lagging behind there, most definitely, but amenities, you couldn't fault.

'Perhaps there's something wrong with me,' I ventured as we munched our way through the cold pizza. 'I don't feel guilty or upset at all,' I added conspiratorially.

'Only you could feel bad about not feeling bad,' said Tash, rolling her eyes.

'I should, though, shouldn't I? Feel awful about Richmond. About getting rid of the bond between me and him. Shouldn't I feel sad and tragic instead of feeling liberated? I feel...I feel straightened out.'

'You should feel as you feel. It's always better to feel good, than to feel bad,' said Tash sagely.

The phone rang and automatically I stiffened, the blood running out of my calves, making them numb with fear. Tash grabbed the phone authoritatively.

'Hello,' she said. 'No. Who's calling please. Just a moment,' and then she put her hand over the receiver. 'A Shock?'

'What?'

'It's A Shock.'

'What is?' I said frowning. Then I started giggling. I held on to the coffee table, laughing hysterically while Tash pursed her lips at me. 'Sorry,' I said, taking the phone from her, putting my hand over the receiver. 'Ashok,' I pronounced like a school teacher, 'Ash-oak.'

Tash made a face and waggled her fingers at me, with her thumb on her nose. 'Who's Ashoak then?'

'Dunno,' I said grinning. 'Hello?'

'Hello,' said a boy's voice, 'is that Mira Chowdhary?'

'Yeah?' I said, raising my eyebrows at Tash.

'Is my dad there, please?'

CHAPTER NINETEEN

'Hello?' said the voice.

'Who's this?'

The voice became overtly formal, stiff. 'This is Ashok Kaushik. I was wondering if you knew where my dad was. Amrit.'

I shot a look at Tash, felt my throat constricting. His child. I was talking to Amrit's child.

'Amrit Kaushik,' insisted the boy, and hearing his name spoken by a child's voice made a knot in my stomach. There was a silence and in those moments I felt myself sinking, dizzy.

'You're Amrit's son?' I said dumbly. Tash was biting the side of her thumb.

'Look, can you tell him...' The voice was impatient now.

'Listen,' I pleaded, 'he's not here. He's not here. How did you get this number? Why are you phoning me?' I could hear my voice rising in panic, trying to wrench myself away.

'It was on the itemized phone bill. I called before and heard your message. That's how I know your name.'

All those phone calls in the middle of the night when his

voice had growled into my ear, so close and private and precious. They were public property, listed in black and white, for children to see. You can't do that, I wanted to shout, you can't know these things.

'I...I don't know what to say to you,' I said miserably. 'He's not here. I promise.'

'Oh,' said Ashok. 'Well, doesn't matter then.' He sounded so young. There was no trace of anger or bitterness in his voice. It shook me.

'What's the trouble, Ashok?'

'He's disappeared hasn't he? He's gone AWOL. Just told us he was leaving. He's always saying he's leaving. Now he's gone.'

He just sounds like a kid, I thought, like all the kids squabbling on the top deck of a bus in the afternoons, piling on top of one another, driving everybody mad with their racket. His accent, it's just London, no trace of Amrit's received pronunciation. An accent just like ours, me and Tash and Frank, full of lazy aitches and dropped consonants and no concession for exorbitant school fees. How strange that I had never known the names of his children.

'He's gone?' I said in disbelief. It was impossible. Amrit wouldn't abandon his children.

'He's not dead,' said Ashok scornfully. 'He phoned up to say he was staying with a friend.'

'Oh.'

'If you see him before Saturday, can you tell him please that the concert begins at twelve and he's got to pick up the ticket by then,' said Ashok tightly.

I wanted to tell him that I wouldn't see Amrit, had nothing to do with this, it wasn't my fault, I wasn't responsible, but the words wouldn't form in my mouth. Christ, you sound just like him, I thought fleetingly. 'I'll tell him. If I see him. I'm sure he'll remember to...'

'Right, 'bye then,' said Ashok and the line went dead.

Tash poured me a whiskey. I was staring at the remains of the pizza on the coffee table, listening to the dialling tone.

'It's alright,' she said, taking the phone away and replacing it. 'Don't get spooked. Kids do all sorts of mad things, don't take it...'

'It's not alright, Tash,' I said. 'It was never alright.'

After fear, came relief. And after relief, there was shame. That was the new country.

'Look,' she said carefully, 'you've just been through an operation. And now you've had a shock.'

Neither of us laughed. Only minutes ago we had been witty, scoring points.

'Tash,' I said, 'do you mind if I go out by myself? I want to take a walk.'

'I'll come with you.'

'No,' I said tightly. 'I can't bear anyone to see me.'

'You need to rest,' she said. 'Stay here. I'll go out.'

'You've got a virus. You'll get a relapse. It's cold outside.'

We looked at each other helplessly. Tash squeezed my hand. I turned my face away from her. Tears rolled down my cheeks. She held my hand and let me cry. 'Everyone knew, Tash.

Everyone knew. I feel so ashamed. It was all so little.'

'You loved someone. You opened your heart. You should be proud not ashamed,' she said.

It's over, it's over, it's over, I told myself.

We turned on the TV again and watched the programmes till it was dark outside. I had never seen so much TV in one sitting. We sat transfixed to the box. There was a comedy and a soap opera and a sitcom and a documentary about jazz music. It ended with a Billie Holiday song, the same song that I had heard so long ago. I had told myself to remember that night when it was over between us.

'I want to do something,' I said.

'What?'

'It's irrational.'

'Naturally.'

'Will you help me?'

'Yes,' she said unreservedly.

I removed the pizza box and glasses from the coffee table and took hold of one end. Tash took hold of the other. We dragged it down the stairs and out to the pathway. Then we carried it towards the series of large council dustbins situated at the side of the block of flats. Someone had stuck up a handwritten notice:

THIS IS NOT A COUNCIL DUMP. PLEASE DO NOT LEAVE TELEVISION SETS, BITS OF FURNITURE OR CONSUMER DURABLES HERE
Signed S. Clarke – chair, Residents Association.

We stared at the notice and looked around for witnesses. The table seemed to weigh a ton. It was a dark silent evening.

'Fuck it,' we both said together. Ashes to Ashes. We dumped the table next to the bins and sprinted back up the stairs like naughty schoolkids.

'Someone's bound to take it away,' she said. 'There's always someone who wants someone else's rubbish.'

The next day, I had to go to work. Mrs Menozzi told me that there was a meeting I had to go to. All the graduates and part-time staff were assembled in the back room and the general manager twitched in his three-piece suit when I pushed open the door. There was an air of disinterest in the room, people lounging and looking out of the window. Connor winked across at me. Nobody was surprised when the manager said that all temporary contracts were to be terminated by the end of the week. Saturday would be our last day, he was sorry but…blah, blah, blah. Nobody cared about his discomfort, they had already started looking for real work, with real wages.

I wondered if Amrit would turn up at the concert to fulfil his obligations. RaviKavi had clambered eagerly to participate in the PTA meetings and sports days and prize-givings and school plays. I used to roll my eyes at their discussions and observations. Get a life, I used to think when I was ten. I didn't think they had a life which didn't centre around me until the

Visiting Gods started to arrive at Heathrow airport. Fat ladies and swarthy men pummelling my face with podgy fingers, exclaiming with surprise at how I'd grown, dispensing tales of my antics as a baby. What a piece of the moon I had been, they'd say, always willing to be entertained by any number of people, leaving RaviKavi free to talk and discuss. They all knew each other's families, asked after someone's cousin's sister-in-law as though they were all connected. They couldn't leave each other alone. I used to stare at them pityingly, those fragments of the past flapping in the London streets. I didn't believe any of them had ever had a real life, not the sort people had in London where they were free from families and honour and restraint and duty and being good. RaviKavi used to hoot with laughter at the American chat shows where children clutched their estranged parents and declared, 'I love you, Mom.' 'I tell you, these programmes are set ups,' my dad would say suspiciously; 'they pay actors.' I remembered Luke telling me not to say that I loved him if I didn't mean it. 'Don't say it like an obligation. Don't say it at all.'

The coffee table was still outside when I got home and I felt inexplicably irritated with the burglars and scavengers of the neighbourhood. Tash had left a note. She had a list of flats and bedsits to see. The front room looked empty, bereft. I thought wildly about hauling the table back inside because it had become such a fixture in the room. I knelt on the sofa and stared out of the window at it down below, next to the bins.

Luke phoned me. He said that Frank had told him I needed cheering up, what was wrong, how great about the book, why hadn't I told him. How decent he is, I thought. How I respect him. Why don't I love him without a feeling of obligation? How was it possible to love somebody you didn't respect, thought shameless? Someone you couldn't introduce to your friends or family, someone you couldn't believe in. But it's not love, I told myself. It's not love, it's a habit, dirty like smoking, automatic like tradition. But nothing is unconquerable. People stopped smoking just like that, in a second of revelation and fear.

'I'm moving out,' said Luke. 'The Oily Rag and the
Sunbeam are looking for a new squat mate.'

I laughed. 'Where will you go?'

'I'm moving in with a friend. I met her in India. She's a
painter but she's teaching French at the Alliance Française.'

Luke had found a girl. Why hadn't it occurred to me
before? It was so perfect and inevitable.

'We're just friends,' he said, answering my unspoken
disappointment. 'At the moment. I want you to meet her.'
There was a silence. 'Are you still...'

'No,' I said. 'That's all over now.'

'Good.'

'I think I know someone,' I said brightly, 'for the room.'

Tash moved in with the Oily Rag and the Sunbeam on
Saturday afternoon. I was at work all day, selling my last hat
and glove. The store was full of large red placards announcing
huge discounts. Some of the temporary staff hadn't bothered to
come in, including Connor. There was no leaving party
planned. I felt a little deflated. Mrs Menozzi wasn't in and
suddenly I felt sad that I hadn't been able to say goodbye. One
of her friends from Gardening Tools said that Mrs Menozzi's
mother, who was in a wheelchair, had hurt her arm and Mrs
Menozzi was at the hospital. I asked him more about her, this
woman who had absently kissed my cheek when I heard the
news about the novel being accepted for publication. In 1958,
Mrs Menozzi had married a waiter who worked in Bar Italia!
He was from the same village in Naples as she was. He had died
of a sudden heart attack at the age of twenty-seven and Mrs
Menozzi's mother had come to live in England. They had
looked after each other since 1968, two old ladies now, with
three cats and one income. It shocked me that after all this time
I knew nothing about her real life, not even her first name. I
hadn't given her a single thought. My last day at the store was
uneventful and I felt my life was going into slow motion. For
the first time I was dreading returning to an empty flat. I didn't
know what I would do with myself.

CHAPTER TWENTY

The table had disappeared! I stared at the empty space on the pavement and my heart leapt with joy. Racing upstairs, taking the steps two at a time, I was bubbling with a sense of freedom. Tash had left a bottle of whiskey and a large packet of cheese and onion crisps in the centre of the carpet where the table had been. She had attached a DRINK ME and EAT ME post-it note on the items. I sat down cross-legged in the middle of the room. Gleefully, I tore open the crisps and started devouring them, shoving handfuls into my mouth and letting crispy smithereens spray out. I broke open the whiskey bottle and poured a fat tumblerful. Then I emptied half the ice tray into it. I'm going to acquire a taste for whiskey, I thought. It was sour stuff but bracing. I took out the telephone directories and looked up Menozzi, then called the number. There was no answer and I put the phone down in disappointment. Well, I thought, maybe I'll stay in and read a book. It was the first Saturday night I had stayed in since I was sixteen! I was definitely growing up. But after half an hour of reading the words were swimming in front of my eyes and I had an irresistible urge to hear his voice. His face loomed up in my mind, bobbing dangerously. If I phoned him, nobody would know. If I just dialled the number and put the phone down, nobody would know. I felt my mouth go dry, my palms broke into a sweat, the lower part of my back ached. I can't let go, not yet, I thought wildly. I'm not ready. I'll just look up the number, he won't be home anyway. I stared miserably at the space outside, next to the rubbish bins, where the table had been. What difference would it make now? Everything was over, wasn't it? There would be no harm done, because there was nothing left. We were friends, weren't we? We were loving friends. I had to hear his voice. Just once. What harm would it do? What happiness I would feel. I threw down my book and rushed to the page in my address book. I swallowed. Gingerly, I reached for the receiver but it rang before I could touch it. My heart lurched.

'Have you drunk the whole bottle?' shouted Tash.

'What?'

'The whiskey.'

'No of course not. What do you think I am, an alcoholic?'

'Good. Get in a cab and come over to the squat. We're having a painting party.'

'Tash,' I said, looking at my watch, 'it's ten o'clock at night.'

'Yeah, so? And you're in on a Saturday night. And it was your last day at work. And you haven't reached middle age just yet.'

'The table's disappeared, Tash,' I said dolefully.

'And after a few more glasses of whiskey, you were going to persuade yourself that it would be alright to speak to him, because now the table's gone, it can't hurt you any more?'

I sighed. 'That was the general idea.'

'Mira,' she said patiently, 'that's kidology, and you know it.'

'Speak English, Oprah,' I said sullenly.

'I've got a better idea. Come over, help us paint the walls, take lots of drugs and trash yourself with us.'

'I don't think so.'

'I've got something to tell you,' she said mysteriously.

'What?'

'It's juicy.'

'What?'

'You have to come round to hear it.'

'Don't piss about.'

'No, it's true. I've got something you'll want to hear. The question is, are you going to let curiosity get the better of you?'

Half an hour later, I was paying the cab driver.

'Hello, sweetheart!' gushed the Sunbeam at the door, hugging me in a mighty embrace. 'You OK?'

My eyes nearly popped out of my head. I had never heard the Sunbeam say more than two words at a time, unless they were to do with his car or motorbike. And the Sunbeam didn't do public demonstrations of affection. He was called the Sunbeam because of his car, but mainly because he was always moaning, scowling and carrying round his disfigurement like a trophy. I followed him suspiciously into the front room. I'd forgotten how large it was. All the furniture had been pushed to the sides and covered with dustsheets and the carpet had been torn out, revealing perfect grainy floorboards, which Tash was in the process of covering with newspaper. There were five pots of Dulux paint on one side of the room.

'I'll go and get you a drink,' smiled the Sunbeam and disappeared into the kitchen.

'Is he on drugs?' I asked Tash.

'Get your overalls on,' she commanded.

'You're serious about this? You only just moved in for chrissakes!' I said, putting on the baggy workman's overalls. I had to hand it to Tash, she had organized the painting party with a vengeance. There was a large collection of fresh paint brushes, ashtrays and cigarette packets next to the paint pots.

'We're feeling energized,' she said and winked at me. 'The real painters are coming first. And the rabble are coming later.'

'Yeah anyway. What's the big secret?'

'Let me see,' she said, tapping her chin with her finger, 'do you want the Big one or the Little one?'

'Tash!' I shouted.

The Sunbeam walked in carrying three glasses and a bottle of wine. He started pouring the wine, a big goofy smile on his face. I stared at him. He looked different somehow. Maybe he'd had a bath.

'Luke's coming too. You don't mind, do you?' said Tash. 'It's about time I met him after all.'

'I'd love to see him,' I said happily.

'He's coming with Emmanuelle,' said the Sunbeam.

'What's she like?' I couldn't help asking.

'She's alright. Quite pretty. Doesn't say much.'

'Hmm,' I said.

'They're just friends,' said the Sunbeam.

'You don't know that,' I said.

'Guys talk. I know.'

'Hmm,' I said with dissatisfaction.

'She's black,' said Tash slyly.

My mouth dropped. 'Really?'

'I thought that would interest you,' she said with a smirk. 'That's the Little one.'

'So what's she like?' I said eagerly and we all started laughing. 'I always thought Luke would have found himself a blonde, an English rose.'

'Well you know how it is. After a while all white women start to look the same,' chuckled the Sunbeam.

'Oh really,' said Tash archly, her hand on her hip.

'Aww,' said the Sunbeam, 'I never even noticed you were white, darling. You're the colour of love.'

I was watching their interaction like a tennis match. The doorbell rang. The Sunbeam got up and left the room.

'Pardon?' I spluttered, staring at Tash.

'And that,' she said, running her fingers through her closely-cropped hair, a smug smile on her face, 'is the Big one.'

Luke and Emmanuelle walked in before I could close my

mouth which had dropped about a mile. She was pretty and petite. She had long thin plaits, trickling down to her waist. Luke came across and hugged me, then he put his arm on his girl's shoulder, she was almost a foot shorter than him.

'This is Emmanuelle,' he smiled.

"Ello, Mira." She said it like a French word. I'd never heard my name sound so chic! I kissed her on both cheeks. I knew I was going to like her.

'Say something in French,' I said childishly.

'What shall I say?' she asked shyly.

'Say: Tash, come into the kitchen right now. You've got a lot of explaining to do,' I laughed.

By 3 a.m. the party was in full flow. Every single person was in some form of drug-induced altered state. The house was vibrating with the noise. The Oily Rag was playing DJ in the back room, where people were dancing flamboyantly around bottles of wine, passing joints, cutting lines. The front room had been unbelievably painted and locked up. People kept arriving in the kitchen with beer and bottles, raising their hands or passing cans overhead. I was wedged against the fridge next to Tash who was whispering to me in a low growl. She and the Sunbeam had been doing the wild thing all day, an hour after she had crossed the threshold! She thought his scar was sexy; did I know his real name was Amir Abdul Nazar Ali, and that he had fifteen muscles in his upper arm? I couldn't stop laughing as she insisted on going into all the graphic details. And in the middle of that crazy loud party, with people's elbows in my face and wine and beer spilling over my shoes and joints dancing across sticky fingers, I caught sight of my reflection in the kitchen window. I was covered with paint, my hair tied back into a scraggy pony tail, my head was thrown back, I was crying with laughter, gasping for breath. I hadn't seen myself so happy for such a long time.

As the months passed, I found myself becoming part of a group. It started with the revelation that Tash and the Sunbeam had fallen in love in the first week of her moving into the squat. Unbelievably, they were going to get married in May. Luke and Emmanuelle had become more than friends. Connor and I saw each other on dates. Neither of us wanted to go out together, have a boring relationship. I told Frank privately that it couldn't last, he was so gorgeous and Irish and had a motorbike and everything, but he seemed to like me. Frank said he was fed up with couples.

For New Year's Eve, I decided it was time that all the friends I had kept in my separate lives finally met each other. It was unavoidable in any case. Two of them were getting married for chrissakes! I organized a dinner in the tapas restaurant in Camden Town and slyly asked the agent Torquil to come too, so that we would be a perfect eight.

'If you go out with him,' I said to Frank, 'he'll be family.'

'I've never had a conversation with the guy,' he said, checking his appearance in the mirror.

'I thought you'd slept with him at least three times.'

'Precisely,' said Frank.

'We'll have champagne and oysters,' I said once everyone had assembled been and introduced to each other. Nobody wanted to have champagne, it was too expensive, and when I offered to pay they all shouted me down.

'We'll have Cava,' said Frank smiling at me, and I knew he was thinking of our funny holiday with the pipe woman and my letter written on the cool tiles of the bathroom, the letter he had warned me not to send for four days.

'No oysters,' declared the Sunbeam, who was allergic to them. Falling in love seemed to have transformed him. He'd shaved off his beard and had a bath. He looked quite presentable.

'You must have them in Galway,' said Connor, 'best oysters on the planet.'

'They're an acquired taste,' said Luke and I said they tasted like kissing someone who hadn't brushed their teeth. Everyone laughed and said we would have mussels in garlic instead, and bread with tomatoes. Tash and I asked Emmanuelle foolish drunken questions about French women and how come they were so thin, and the boys talked about football and how come girls never stopped talking. It was one of those times when without any premeditation, confessions and revelations swam around the table. The sort of rare times when people feel safe and sound and nothing seems to be difficult, everything needs to be said and things are understood without being said. These rare moments in our lives when we shift closer to each other imperceptibly.

Oddly, it was Emmanuelle who started it, the stranger amongst us. She said she had a maniacal fear of failure, of her paintings never amounting to anything. We assured her they would and one day she would make a painting which would be the front cover of a book I would write about the eight of us talking rubbish in a tapas bar in Camden Town. It led to us talking about our fears. Luke said he had tried to eat turnips and spinach because he thought he should leave behind those childhood fears and then realized that some fears weren't worth the bother of conquering. We all said it was totally possible to live without touching those vegetables. The Sunbeam said he was afraid of nothing, now he'd met the woman of his dreams. We all swooned and groaned.

'Make sure you get the car in the divorce,' said Frank. 'Make him write it down.'

'The car's the thing,' giggled Luke.

'She's not having the car,' warned the Sunbeam.

'You need that car, Tash,' said Connor.

'What's his is yours,' chuckled Torquil.

'No way. I grew up with that car,' protested the Sunbeam.

'Get the car!' we all shouted.

'I want the car,' said Tash in a dramatic solemn voice, looking at her husband-to-be.

The Sunbeam reached over and kissed her. 'You got it baby,' he said.

'Yes!' we all screamed, slapping our palms together high above the table.

The clock chimed midnight and the whole restaurant

exploded into cheers and whistles punctuated by the popping Cava corks. From somewhere a corny Scottish version of 'For Auld Lang Syne' started up, and almost everybody in the restaurant screamed with disgust. We àll leant over and kissed each other and there was a huge 'hurray' in the restaurant when the recording was aborted halfway through a particularly nauseating phrase.

We all raised our glasses to Tash and the Sunbeam, said they had to promise not to turn into boring people who watched TV and only went out with couples. Even when they had babies. And then Frank poured himself another glass of Cava and spoke silently so that we all hushed up our shouting to hear him.

'I've always wanted a child, ever since I was sixteen years old. My fear is that I'll go through life never knowing what it is to be a dad,' he declared and I understood the silence in which we had travelled back from the clinic.

'You need to get yourself a broody girlfriend,' said Tash. 'It doesn't matter if you're gay, all sorts of people have families.'

'You can come and babysit my godson. Anytime. That'll beat motherhood out of you,' flirted Torquil.

And what did I say about my fears? I said I was afraid of the dark. Everyone laughed and said everybody was afraid of the dark, but once you stayed in the dark and got used to the geography of the place it was a cinch to come out to the light.

We all drank and smoked excessively and felt like grown-ups and children at the same time, giggling and at ease with each other. Conversations rambled around the table, stopping off halfway, cross cut by each other. From time to time, I looked across at one of my friends talking animatedly about a subject and I wondered if the pain would come back, the pain of Amrit gone. Yet, there was such joy in that restaurant that night, the exhilaration of connections being made that I knew I was living through something important. I didn't know if I was alive, but I knew there was activity around me, furious life, skins and smells and laughter.

We started to meet for coffee and have dinner together frequently. Tash and I took Emmanuelle to the Everyman to see French films and gossiped about Luke. Does he still have cold feet in bed? Nobody had much money yet we found things to do together, because we were a unit now. Everybody was buoyed up by the prospect of my book coming out, as though it was an event that made us part of something. The launch party was just weeks away.

Into this happy fray, RaviKavi arrived back from India, the house in Delhi still unfinished. They said they felt like tourists in London now, tourists with roots. In the weeks leading up to the launch, there was a frenetic activity in my world. Everybody kept phoning me up to ask the same questions, or just to ask if I was excited or just to talk. I enjoyed it immensely, this feeling of camaraderie that had come out of nowhere, without any effort. I revelled in my life being braided with their lives and I thought of how lucky I was to be so close and near and driven to distraction by the ones I loved. I remembered the Visiting Gods and how I had resented them, and now I understood why it hadn't mattered to RaviKavi that their poetry books had been pilfered so shamelessly, their hospitality taken for granted. They had always known that friendships were about rights over people, that love was fierce. That people who had thrown in their lot with each other were responsible and accountable to each other. In those days leading up to the launch of the book, I learnt how much I depended on those close to me, how theirs was the only approbation I sought. I realized that dependence is not always a hindrance. Sometimes it could be one's only support.

The publisher who was footing the bill for the launch nearly had a heart attack when he saw my list. I'd invited Tash's mum and the Burly Spaniard, Frank's mum and dad, Ralph and Matty, Mrs Menozzi, both of Connor's brothers who were in London for the weekend. I thought about sending Amrit an invitation and then decided against it. It was better to leave things the way they were. I didn't think he would come in any case and I didn't want to be looking over my shoulder the whole evening. I had often wondered what we had been to each other. And what we could have been. And then I had thought of all the improper secrets between us, the secrets which had changed me, changed me in a way I would find out later in my life. Nothing was broken, the woman at the clinic had told me. Go on, go on with your life. Nothing was broken, but something had gone, finished, and the space where it had existed would always be there.

The publisher stared at the list in horror, and then at me. 'The idea of a book launch is to get publicity,' he said. 'It's not a shebeen. We have to invite journalists and reviewers. Can't you cut it down?'

'Well,' I said, 'no, I can't. These are family and friends and then these are the family of friends and then, well these are just people I like and who'd love to come. You see people would get offended.'

The publisher muttered that even top-selling authors didn't have such a huge list.

'Don't worry,' I said enthusiastically. 'They'll all fit in.'

The launch of the book fell on the snowiest day recorded in February for fifty years. The publisher was depressed because journalists wouldn't bother to tramp up to another book launch, of an unknown writer, in that sort of weather. I couldn't care less. I was rather pleased. It seemed ridiculous to be passing myself off as a writer at the age of twenty-five. On the night of the launch, Frank took me out for an early dinner.

'You know when I came to Richmond?' he said.

'Why were you in such a mood?' I said. 'I think I'll have this. How do you pronounce it? Zarzuela. I'll have that. Sounds exotic.'

'I was just... You're like my sister. I was worried,' he said.

'Oh,' I said and smiled.

'You always make people feel they must look after you,' he

said, slanting his eyes as though it was a trick I played.

'What?' I said aghast. 'Like I'm a whuss?'

'No. Because you...Because you just barge into things. You don't think about it, you rush in.'

'I don't think I...' I stopped as the waitress deposited my plate of food. 'What the hell's that?' I said, staring at the bulbous contents.

Frank started laughing. I poked around with my fork and lifted some to my mouth.

'It's not terrible,' I said, making a face.

'Just leave it. Order some chicken. Don't try and be so adventurous.'

'OK,' I said and ordered chicken.

'Are you alright?'

'Yes,' I said and thought it over. 'Yes, I'm alright.'

'No ghosts?'

'Some.'

'Give it time.'

'Yes,' I said.

When we arrived at the book launch in the restaurant we were confronted by a thick crowd. The corner by the door was piled high with coats and umbrellas and boots. The publisher was smiling so there must have been a few journalists there. Tash and the Sunbeam, Luke and Emmanuelle were circulating as instructed, behaving properly as I had hoped they would. It wasn't like the last time I had been to a literary launch and shyly plucked a glass of champagne to steady my nerves. Here, there was a noisy corner.

It was full of middle-aged Indians talking at the top of their voices. Despite my strict instructions, RaviKavi had invited all the people they knew in London to make up for the fact that none of my family from India could be there. They were huddled in a corner, the men with raised glasses, standing in tight uncomfortable suits and many of the women arranged happily on chairs taken without asking from the elegant food table. I had insisted on sheek kebabs, chicken tikka, samosas

and onion bhajiis. 'You don't understand,' I had explained to
my bewildered publisher who had planned on peanuts and
crisps. 'You can't invite Indian people to a party without any
proper food, there'll be a riot. It's simply not done.'

All the Indians had paper plates loaded with 'snakes' as
they guffawed and shouted proprietorially at each other. My
dad was a little drunk and I rolled my eyes at Frank who was
laughing his head off.

'I am the author's father,' he said proudly to a bemused
journalist. 'Have a samosa, they're really very good.'

'Nightmare,' I hissed at Frank.

There was a huge 'Oohhh' as I approached the Indian
society and several white people jumped out of their skin.
'Hello, hello,' shouted their friends as they claimed me under
the canopy of their outstretched hands. A few of the aunties
took hold of my cheeks between finger and thumb, as
though I was ten years old. I escaped in the crowd, searching
for one of my well-behaved friends who kept winking or
putting their thumbs up to me in the crowd. I looked at the
pile of books sitting at the table next to the food. I knew none
of the aunties and uncles would buy the book, they would
borrow, they would fight over who borrowed first, or
demand gratis copies. I was smiling at the prospect of this as
my gaze moved across the bobbing heads. A long time ago,
I had looked through a crowd and seen a man talking to a
girl and felt a whole catalogue of emotions for that stranger.
I had run away, unable to comprehend what was happening.

'I'm going to the shop for ciggies,' I whispered to Frank
who was chatting to a group of people I didn't know. I
pushed my way to the door and a chilly gust of wind made
me catch my breath. The snow was falling steadily in fat
white flakes. I trudged down the road, making thick imprints
in the snow. Everybody was here and yet I felt sad and
empty. Would it always be like this, wanting to be part of the
good strong things and at the same time wishing to be
outside them?

Soho Square was two streets away. I couldn't resist it. I

wanted to see it in the snow. I walked along, puffing on my cigarette. The sky was a pale grey. The square was empty and covered with unblemished thick snow. I ran up one of the pathways, towards the central construction, which looked like a little snowhouse. I sat down heavily on the bench where Charles the second must have sat with his mistress and surveyed the scene. Everything was still, the buildings etched out with charcoal, the black imprints of my boots on the pathway. There wasn't a soul in sight, but my head was thrumming with memories. I stared at the swirling white particles suspended in the air. A long time ago, I had stretched out on the grass, wet and green, wanting to live and live, felt myself soaring up into the sky. I remembered grinning at Amrit in the Despair, intent on acquiring new habits and experiences and ideas. As I sat huddled and alone in the middle of Soho Square, suddenly I knew that I had crossed an impasse. I had begun to defend and protect the things in my life that previously I had scorned. Automatically, I closed my palms over my nose and took a deep breath and inhaled the irresistible scent of musk. Kastoori, that was the Hindi word for musk. A great rush of emotion came over me. I realized I had a past. I wasn't just alive. I had lived. I had seen things. I was connected to people. The journey had only just begun.

I got up and began walking back to the launch party, increasing my pace as I approached the street. Little snowflakes settled on the edge of my nose and I wriggled my face till they fell into watery drops down my cheek. I looked around when I was at the door. Perhaps he'll come, I thought fleetingly, perhaps he'll pass by and say, oh, I was just passing. Somebody had put up a sign saying PRIVATE PARTY. Snow was falling relentlessly in the empty street. Everybody who was supposed to be here had arrived. I pushed open the door and went inside.

CHAPTER TWENTY-ONE

Unlike fashionable famous people, I was the last to leave the launch party. Connor and I stayed behind to help the waitresses clear up. Then we sat down and had a few drinks with them in the empty restaurant. I had a distinct feeling of anticlimax. Here I am, I thought, so safe and intact, with a gorgeous boy and a pile of books and my heart is heavy. What do you want, Luke had asked me once. All I knew then was I wanted more. Now, I thought sheepishly, perhaps I wanted a little less. Was there no end to yearning? Connor said he would drive me home and not come in. He thought I wanted to be alone. I thought so too, but I couldn't sleep. I took out the bottle of whiskey that Tash had left, and slowly poured myself a peg. When the phone rang at two in the morning, I knew instinctively who the caller was, even though I had not seen him for six months.

'I'm sorry it's so late,' he said slowly. 'I was in North London, I thought I would give you a call. As friends.'

I felt the familiar tedious rushing of blood around my veins. 'I heard you'd disappeared, some months ago,' I said evenly.

'I went to stay with Ralph in Brighton. I just wanted to get away for a while.' He paused. 'I had a notion that I might change my life,' he said and then laughed, embarrassed, as though he had said something childish.

'Uh-huh,' I said, surprised at the calmness in my voice.

'I locked myself in the spare room, with a bottle of whiskey. And a good book.' He paused, and continued in his maddening casual tone. 'I believe the book has just been published. The writer is an impossibly glamorous young person.'

I couldn't help smiling at the phone.

'Hello?' he said uncertainly.

'Hello,' I said.

'I've returned like a bad penny,' he said with a hollow chuckle. 'Did you call the university?'

'One of your children phoned me.'

He sighed. 'I'm sorry. I'm sorry about that. Mira, I'm not such a terrible person as you think. I try and do my best. I went to the concert if you're interested.'

'I bet you were late and you spent the whole day reading the book reviews in *The Times*,' I said.

'No, I was good. I watched and clapped and talked with the other parents. My son is turning into a rather good performer. I was useless at music when I was young.'

'It was a shock,' I said and laughed. I couldn't help myself. 'Do you remember *The Far Pavilions* on the TV?'

'A. Shock and his beautiful browned-up princess. Yes. I wrote a few pompous articles about that.'

I rolled my eyes.

'My other son is called Ajay. He's only seven. He said to me the other day that he was going to change his name to Ajoy, pretend he was really a Bengali. They'd been studying Bangladeshi communities in the East End at school. He said, "My friends will think I'm a joy to be with."'

We both laughed.

'Where are you?' I said.

'In Camden Town,' he said miserably and the nearness of

his geographical location pumped the blood around my arteries with a renewed vigour.

'Why did you run away?' he said in a small voice. 'I waited for you. I was worried about you. I didn't know where you'd gone. You shouldn't have walked out on me like that.'

I smiled at the routine. I was worried about you, I mimicked inside my head. That was my cue to collapse. I'd seen it so often, believed it so often. It suddenly occurred to me that so many times we had met and talked to each other, made love or held hands, but the only time that I felt he was himself, really himself, was when he was like this: separated from me, talking at a distance, almost having a conversation with himself, sloshing around in his own pool of self-pity. And I, I was like a screen on which he projected his disgust with himself. And then it would be over. He would check himself and make a joke or a clever remark, thus making me into a girl and himself into a philanderer, roles we both played and lived off. It was a strange and exotic place where he took us, every time we embraced. A place where neither of us could help or reach the other. The only solution was to run. Run like hell.

'Well, you know,' I said breezily, 'things to do, people to see.'

There was a silence. Then he said, 'Would you like some company? I used to amuse you.'

I felt I had grown tired of my responses. I had a strange feeling of boredom.

'Look at me,' he said, as though I could see through the telephone. 'I'm a decrepit old man, wandering down the side of the road. Along with the rest of the down and outs.'

'Oh dear,' I said. 'Are we feeling sorry for ourselves?'

'Yes, we are,' he said.

I hesitated. I knew he wouldn't beg. Amrit would never plead. Just as he would never say more than he had about reading my book. He would stiffen his upper lip. I could do it now. I could refuse him and it would cut like a knife. I could have revenge. But revenge for what?

'Come and see me then. Hop in a cab,' I said.

'Thank you,' he said. 'I'll get you some cigarettes. You're bound to have run out.'

I wanted to cling on to righteousness. I'd never liked those Sita women, they forgave too much, suffered endlessly. They were door matty's. I raced over his telephone words uttered on the side of a street, coolly assessing how much on his knees he was. The larger his despair, the greater my satisfaction; it filled me like food. I imagined him pressing the bell over and over like a character from an old black and white movie while I sat upstairs, imperious and waterproof. I wanted to relish it, his temporary lapse into human emotion, stamp upon it as hard as I could.

And then a strange thing happened.

I was staring at myself in the mirror when I heard his voice again, as though he was in the room. I turned sharply towards the upturned phone and pressed it gingerly to my ear. Somehow, his mobile had not turned itself off. What outrageous fortune! I had been given the chance to be the invisible man.

'Will you go North?' he was saying.

'Not on my way, sir,' said the taxi driver.

'Please,' he said. 'It would mean a lot to me.' I had never heard Amrit say please. I had never heard his voice so small. As soon as he had settled himself he struck up a conversation with the driver, who I immediately realized was Asian.

'Do you get much trouble, in your cab?' he asked.

'Oh, you know what the English people are like, saab.'

'Bloody racist thugs,' said Amrit. 'I used to drive a taxi, many years ago. There was always terrible trouble.'

I stared incredulously at the phone. Amrit who had been trained by a Christian lady on the finer aspects of English etiquette, who had watched the melting CUNT in Cambridge, who knew which Chardonnay to pick out, had never in his life driven a taxi, I was sure. And yet, here he was, ingratiating himself to an ordinary man. For some reason, my heart palpitated and softened unbearably at the unfolding of such a stupid, stupendous lie. I felt a sudden desire to not listen, to let him be, but I couldn't cut him off.

'Ah, it's a long time I've been here. I've seen too much,' said the driver.

'It's too long to be away from home,' said Amrit.

'My wife, she is still in my village with my children. I came here sixteen years ago and look at me, I don't own a thing. I live in a stinking room in Deptford, do this menial job. I drink pints in the pub. I eat out of takeaways, suffering the humiliation of threats. The scum, they vomit and use abusive language. They have no shame. It is no life. But, saab, what am I saying? You will excuse me.'

'Bhaisaab, you must have courage. It requires courage to continue with things,' said Amrit.

'I have lost all my courage, saab. All I wish now is that I should finish things properly. I would like to go back to my village and lie down in a small place. I would like to die where I was born.'

'Yes,' said Amrit, 'one comes to a point when death is the only thing to look forward to.'

Then there was some sort of fracas, I couldn't make it out. I dug the receiver more urgently into my ear. Curses. Scuffling. Windows being slid shut. A swish of clothes. I imagined that the gaping phone must be lodged inside Amrit's jacket pocket, thudding against the side of the cab as he shifted in his seat.

'Peh,' said the driver, 'rubbish, rubbish everywhere. Soon you'll be home. Safe and sound. Very nice locality. Important people live here, eh?'

'Yes,' said Amrit, 'VIPs.'

And then the phone whirred and turned itself off, its battery finally dead. I sat in my empty room waiting for him. I felt something turning in me. What was it Tash had said? It's always better to feel good than to feel bad.

When he arrived, I peeked at his distorted face through the spyhole. He pressed his nose against the door. I laughed out loud and opened the door suddenly and he pretended to fall in.

'You're different,' he said squinting at me. 'What's happened? What's different about you?'

For a moment I froze. It shows, I thought silently appalled. Only Frank and Tash knew, not even Connor. I had told nobody about Richmond. Then my muscles relaxed. People did this trick all the time, all over the place. They carried their past on their shoulders and behind their eyes, and nobody could tell. He couldn't tell. There was no evidence on my face of cruel acts.

'I'm being nice to you,' I said politely.

He strode past me into the front room holding his nose in the air. I followed him in.

'The table's gone,' he said and sat down heavily on the sofa. He was looking at me in that endless way. I smiled into his eyes gently. He frowned at the whiskey bottle. 'Are you resorting to hard liquor?' he said dryly.

I laughed. 'I've developed a taste for it,' I said, pouring out the remaining liquid into two glasses. We looked at each other and grinned. In another time and another place we might be friends, I thought suddenly. I'd thought forgiveness was a long hard road. I didn't think you could skateboard along it. I remembered the Billie Holiday song I had heard, and how astonished I had been that things could happen in a flash. We sat in silence for a while. I smoked. He didn't.

Finally he spoke. 'I've always loved to sit here and have a drink and listen to you. That's always been true, you know?'

'Yes,' I said, 'I know.'

He sighed and stretched out his legs. 'At the beginning, it was different. It was like a challenge. I couldn't believe my luck. Then it changed. We were into something. It was unexpected. I didn't want to see it. You're right about me. There's something missing inside. It doesn't mean I'm nobody. I work and find happiness in things, but I hurt people. I keep doing it over and over.'

'The kind of person you are,' I said, 'a person who sees the world as a comedy, because you think and don't feel, don't you wonder sometimes, how you became this way? This type of person, this configuration of emotions and actions? Don't you wonder about it?'

He thought it over. 'It bores me,' he said. 'I've tried. I've thought I should.' He grinned. 'I find myself rather uninteresting.'

I started to laugh and he looked at me strangely. 'Have I made a joke?'

'No, it's not funny. It's ironic.'

'How do you mean?'

'Do you think we need things to believe in? Ideas, countries, gods? Do you think those devotees massing on the steps of the temples in India don't know the idols are just clay and paint? Don't they know that it is their faith, their love, which makes the idols live?'

'Yes,' he said, 'they must realize it, on some level.'

'Then it's true.'

'What?'

'We need to believe. Even when we know beyond a shadow of doubt that what we believe in is an illusion.'

Amrit frowned. 'I don't understand you,' he said. 'I'm not being deliberately obtuse, or difficult. I just don't understand the things you say. Things are as they are. One lives. One looks at mountains and sunsets. One shoulders responsibilities. One works. That's about all. What are you thinking? Why have you got such a disapproving look on your face?'

I laughed. 'I'm always disapproving of you.'

'Yes,' he said and scowled like a little boy.

'I have a right to disapprove,' I said lightly, 'because I love you.'

'I wish you didn't. You're determined to love me. I find it astonishing.'

'Yes, I see that now. You are full of astonishment. Maybe you should write a poem at those times.'

He roared with laughter and I laughed too. I remembered that little round table in the Despair and his jowly friends, dreaming of India, talking of Yeats. Knights in rusting armour. I found the scene a little absurd and a little heartrending at the same time. There are always two sides to a story my mum had said.

'I'm no poet,' he said.

'You're a good driver,' I said. 'Poets are terrible drivers. I grew up with poets.'

He rubbed his eyes with his fists like a little boy. Then he leant his head against my shoulder and spoke into the darkness of my skin. 'I wish I could love you the way...in the proper way,' he said and smiled ruefully.

Instinctively, I pressed my hand on his head, the same way he had once laid his upon mine and I had wanted it to stay there always, like a hat against harm.

'You would never have tolerated me you know, the way I am. You would never have made a peace with yourself. There would have been terrible troubles between us. And eventually, you would have left me.'

'You'd better go,' I said, taking my hand away.

There would always be improper secrets between us, threatening to bring us back together. I felt afraid. I wanted to run, as fast as my feet would take me, never looking back, keeping going till I reached solid ground.

'Remember me,' he said all of a sudden. 'Don't forget our brief history together.'

'I thought you wanted me to forget, banish you from my world. In that time when we were sailing without plans,' I grinned.

'I lied.'

'You!' I said and started laughing. 'Surely not! Lies? You never lie. You are good and honest and truthful. A decent man. An example to young persons like me who don't know anything about the world.'

'You have become quite unbearable. A disrespectful girl. No manners at all.'

'Go home.'

'Yes,' he said, suddenly serious. 'It's time for me to leave.'

At the door I looked at him uncertainly. 'Are you alright?'

'Of course. Of course,' he said with a broad smile.

'Shall I call you a cab or something?'

'I shall arrange my own transportation, thank you,' he said.

'Well, goodbye,' I said, a lump in my throat.

We looked at each other at the threshold. I knew I would never again feel his skin on mine, the touch of his breath in the hollow of my neck.

'I suppose I should say we shall always be fond friends,' he said.

'Yes,' I said. 'You should say that.'

I watched him walking down the path. At first the path was bright under the lights and then it grew dark as it disappeared into the road beyond.

READ MORE IN PENGUIN

In every corner of the world, on every subject under the sun. Penguin represents quality and variety—the very best in publishing today.

For complete information about books available from Penguin—including Puffin, Penguin Classics and Arkana—and how to order them, write to us at the appropriate address below. Please note that for copyright reasons the selection of books varies from country to country.

In India: Please write to *Penguin Books India Pvt. Ltd. 11, Community Centre, Panchsheel Park, New Delhi, 110017*

In the United Kingdom: Please write to *Dept JC, Penguin Books Ltd. Bath Road, Harmondsworth, West Drayton, Middlesex, UB7 ODA, UK*

In the United States: Please write to *Penguin Putnam Inc., 375 Hudson Street, New York, NY 10014*

In Canada: Please write to *Penguin Books Canada Ltd. 10 Alcorn Avenue, Suite 300, Toronto, Ontario M4V 3B2*

In Australia: Please write to *Penguin Books Australia Ltd. 487, Maroondah Highway, Ring Wood, Victoria 3134*

In New Zealand: Please write to *Penguin Books (NZ) Ltd. Private Bag, Takapuna, Auckland 9*

In the Netherlands: Please write to *Penguin Books Netherlands B.V., Keizersgracht 231 NL-1016 DV Amsterdam*

In Germany: Please write to *Penguin Books Deutschland GmbH, Metzlerstrasse 26, 60595 Frankfurt am Main, Germany*

In Spain: Please write to *Penguin Books S.A., Bravo Murillo, 19-I'B, E-28015 Madrid Spain*

In Italy: Please write to *Penguin Italia s.r.l., Via Felice Casati 20, I-20104 Milano*

In France: Please write to *Penguin France S.A., 17 rue Lejeune, F-31000 Toulouse*

In Japan: Please write to *Penguin Books Japan, Ishikiribashi Building, 2-5-4 Suido, Tokyo 112*

In Greece: Please write to Penguin Hellas Ltd, dimocritou 3, GR-106 71 Athens

In South Africa: Please write to *Longman Penguin Books Southern Africa (Pty) Ltd, Private Bag X08, Bertsham 2013*